the Silence

Buried in the Silence

Connie Sampson

NeWest Press
Edmonton

Canadian Cataloguing in Publication Data

Sampson, Connie, 1941-
Buried in the Silence

ISBN 0-920897-85-1
1. Nerland, Carney Milton—Trials, litigation, etc.
2. Trials (Murder)—Saskatchewan—Prince Albert.
3. Discrimination in criminal justice administration—
Saskatchewan. I. Title.
KE229.N47S25 1995   345.7124'02523'089973   C95-910505-0
KF224.N47S25 1995

Editor for the Press: Maggie Siggins
Editorial Coordinator: Eva Radford
Cover design: Brenda Burgess
Book design: John Luckhurst / GDL

NeWest Press gratefully acknowledges the financial assistance of The Canada Council; The Alberta Foundation for the Arts, a beneficiary of the Lottery Fund of the Government of Alberta; and The NeWest Institute for Western Canadian Studies.

Printed and bound in Canada by Best Book Manufactures

NeWest Publishers Limited
Suite 310, 10359 - 82 Avenue
Edmonton, Alberta T6E 1Z9

In Memory
of
Leo LaChance

Contents

Acknowledgements

Many people contributed information for this book. I appreciate their efforts. Maggie Siggins has been my mentor and editor. My husband, Keith, and friends Gail Seymour, Laurie Zelinski, and Marty Popescul read and reread the manuscript and gave honest, helpful views. NeWest Press gave me an opportunity. The Canada Council Explorations program offered a grant and encouragement. The staffs of the Prince Albert *Daily Herald,* the Cuelenaere Library, and Computer Answers were generous with their assistance.

Without the difficult work and courage of the LaChance family, especially David and Sandra, the book would not be. Without the patient gift of teaching by elder Adam Constant, the beginning of my understanding would not be. I thank you all.

Leo LaChance, age 15, 1957

CHAPTER ONE

The Man

On 9 April 1993 in Prince Albert, Saskatchewan, white supremacist Carney Nerland sat before a commission of inquiry into the death of Leo LaChance, a Cree from the nearby Big River Reserve. Nerland wore slacks, a sports jacket, and a shirt and tie. He was well-groomed and well-mannered, earnest, intelligent, polite, and helpful. When asked about the man he had confessed to shooting, Nerland told the commission, "I apologize. I really don't remember the gentleman." The killing, after all, had occurred twenty-seven months earlier.

28 January 1991

Saskatchewan in January is cold. Arctic cold. Murderously cold. Even the sun is not anxious to be out for long. On this Monday morning, schoolchildren from the Big River Reserve, sometimes called the White-fish Reserve, trudged to the road to catch the *Se Se Wah Hum* school bus. They leave in the dark and they return home in the dark. The sun, it seems, has had enough of the bone-gnawing cold by the time the children get out of school. It will be gone by suppertime.

As they waited for the school bus, two older boys kicked at lumps of snow and shoved each other to get at the biggest ones. A glow of headlights appeared from the other side of the hill. "Come on, Stupid," one of the bigger boys yelled. One little boy paid no attention. He was kneeling in the driveway, sweeping his hands in rhythmic semicircles through the fresh snow while singing a tuneless little song. "Come *on!*" the oldest boy growled. The school bus screeched to a stop and the door clunked open. The children bounded on board. David LaChance swung the door shut and the bus crunched down the frozen ·dirt road.

In minutes, it swung into the school yard and rolled to a halt near the building. The boys pushed their way off the bottom step, yelling and starting to run. The younger boys paused a second and then raced off in an imitation of Superman. The girls hugged their books to their chests and trudged toward the school. David LaChance walked to the back of the bus, checking for forgotten items. Somebody always bounded back onto the bus in a panic to find an item left behind. "My book, my book!" he will shout, grabbing it from David's hand and trotting off the bus to get back to the other boys, to scramble and shove in the snow by the fence, before the bell rings.

David climbed into the driver's seat and took the bus back toward the junction. His wife, Madeline, saw the bus bump into their driveway before it swung in a wide arc to stop behind the house. Madeline and David had lots to do that day so she had his tea ready.

Across the road, Leo LaChance had finished his breakfast of bannock and rabbit and was tidying up. Leo did not mind getting up early in the morning. He always got up early when he was going trapping, not that there was a point any more. Prices were down and there was little demand for furs. Still, he enjoyed trapping. That was what he did, and so he continued, selling a few pelts now and then for spending money. Today he planned to sell some pelts in Prince Albert: four squirrels and a couple of weasels, worth maybe five dollars in total. Nothing really. But Leo did not need much. He had food and a warm house. He had family and friends. He hunted a little and visited people. That was all he wanted. He no longer had any ambition to do more. He was a contented man in his own way.

Leo's place is a small, tidy, white framed cabin, situated at the southeast entrance to the reserve, a short way up the hill from the junction of two gravel roads. To the left of the house is the road from

Debden, which runs west for ten miles and descends in gentle roller coaster swoops, until it meets the main road of the reserve. The roads are rough washboards, and a vehicle with the springs of a locomotive would be useful when they are dry. A Sherman tank would be useful when they are wet.

Leo's home looks like a child's drawing of a house. It has two windows, one large, one small, on either side of the front door, like so many other small houses on reserves everywhere in western Canada. It has a big open room with a kitchen at one end and a living room at the other, with a short hall leading to a bathroom and the bedrooms. It is heated by a big, square, wood burning stove in the living room. He had a handmade table and chairs, a radio Roseanne had bought him for five dollars, a couch, and a bed. Poverty does not lend itself to fancy furnishings. These few possessions were all Leo had.

From his front windows, Leo could see the back of brother David's pool hall and gas pump, located at the junction. Across the main road, hidden by trees, was David's house. Their father's place is farther up the slope from Leo's.

Leo, at forty-eight, was the youngest of the three surviving LaChance brothers. Albert was the oldest at sixty-two, and David then was fifty-seven. Roseanne, two years younger than Leo, is a widow who lives in Alberta, on the Saddle Lake Reserve. David and Albert's father, David LaChance, died when they were children. Their mother, Agnes, later married her former husband's brother, Dick LaChance. Together, Dick and Agnes added Samerie, Roseanne, Leo, and Virginia to the LaChance family.

Leo and his brothers could build houses like theirs easily. Just a year before, David and Leo had built a log house far back in the bush behind Leo's place. It was on a ridge overlooking the lake, in the same meadow where their family house once was. Leo had twenty or thirty traps and snares laid through the bush from his house up to that meadow. Their home had been behind a screen of trees, overlooking Big River (which is not very big) and Keg Lake. Leo chuckled whenever he thought about that log house they had built. He and David cut the logs there and let them cure for one year. Then they built the cabin, big, sturdy and square, properly chinked, but without a roof as yet. That lack did not worry Leo because the cabin had been built primarily to stall another man who wanted to build on that piece of land. Next year, maybe, he and David would put on a good roof to finish the cabin.

The brothers were fond of each other and met almost daily. Roseanne visited them occasionally, and the brothers stayed in touch with her by telephone. Leo was easy going and pleasant company, and he had a good sense of humour. He liked to stay close to his family.

Leo's eleven-year-old daughter, Candace, lives on the reserve, and although he did not live with her, her mother, Mary Ann, encouraged the closeness between father and daughter. When Candace was a baby, Mary Ann took her to Leo's house and told him he was welcome to visit his child and be a father to her. After that, Leo visited his daughter whenever he could.

Mary Ann and Leo met at the hotel in Debden one evening in 1980 and then moved in together for six months. Mary Ann remembers him as a good man, fun to be with, happy and quiet, who enjoyed trapping, reading, or watching television. Together they would check his trapline and together they would go to Prince Albert to shop, visit, or party. Mary Ann kept Leo's house tidy and immaculate. They were happy together and really only had one argument — when Leo was jealous over the attentions paid to Mary Ann by another man. But eventually they drifted apart. When Candace was born a few months later, however, a new kind of friendship developed between Mary Ann and Leo.

Pay day on a reserve, when social assistance cheques from the Department of Indian Affairs are distributed, occurs every two weeks. Leo received the standard amount for a single person: $74.00 biweekly, or $148.00 per month. He spent much of his money on Candace, bringing her food, clothing, and her favourite junk foods for a treat. Sometimes he brought something for Mary Ann, and, when she married, for her husband, Martin. The two men got along well, and Leo sometimes stayed with the couple and his daughter for a few days at a time.

He was at their house at Christmas, a month before he died. Besides the jacket and mittens he always gave Candace, he gave her a watch and she loved it. But things were not the same that Christmas. Usually Leo loved to joke and laugh, but that year was different. Mary Ann remembers that he was unusually quiet and edgy. He could not sleep at night and would prowl around the house until early morning, when Mary Ann would get up and make breakfast for him. Then he would sleep for a short while. He was concerned that Canada would become involved in the Gulf War and that the government would want young men from the reserve to fight in it.

But Mary Ann believes that much more was worrying him than a foreign war. He told her during that visit he would be "going away" soon and that he wanted her and Candace to have his house. He would not say when or where he was going or if he meant a trip or something else. He just seemed to sense something. Mary Ann believes it is not unusual for Indian people to be aware of their impending death. Certain events and feelings can be interpreted as a warning to prepare for death. Most heed the warning and organize their affairs. Some hold a thanksgiving feast to give thanks for their many years. Friends and relatives are invited and gifts are given. Personal belongings are distributed. Leo was trying to provide for his daughter by making it known she was to have his house. He had nothing else.

Roseanne LaChance heard from Leo several times before his death and she was also aware of his fear, but she could not get him to identify it. He used to telephone his sister several times a year, but that fall of 1990 Leo called her more frequently, often in the middle of the night. He was upset and afraid of something, but he could not tell her. Not on the phone. When they saw each other, they would talk, he said. Roseanne did not see him alive again.

In the morning of 28 January 1991, as Leo got ready for his trip to Prince Albert, he listened to the radio news – the Gulf War was still dominating the airwaves. What were they fighting about? Leo wondered. Didn't they like their leaders? Were there just too many people in a small country? What really bothered him were the wounded, starving, and dying children. That should not happen to little kids.

By late morning, he was ready to pick up supplies at the store in Victoire, and check for mail for the family. Victoire is part of the reserve, but it has been severed by various land sales over the years, so that now it lies a few miles south of the reserve like a tiny island that has drifted away. It is situated at a junction of the main north-south road through the reserve, the road that passes by Leo's house, and a provincial road that leads east to Debden. The store, set back on the west side of the main road, looks more like a hotel than a store. Annexes have been added at random. It is dimly lit inside, and its various merchandise has been fitted into the oddities of its shape. Catercorner to the store is a small white church with a large cemetery behind it and a few houses scattered near the crossroad. Victoire is a small, but essential, island.

David LaChance was disgusted when he learned later that someone had taken Leo to Victoire to the store that morning and that his brother had purchased Lysol. Lysol, mixed with water, is a poor man's wine.

After he returned home, Leo puttered around for a bit, then ate lunch. Before he left on his last trip to Prince Albert, he wrote a note and propped it up on the table. Then he was ready to leave for town and, he hoped, some happy times.

CHAPTER TWO

The Day

28 January 1991

By midafternoon it was still minus twenty-four degrees Celsius. Leo put on a sweater and a long blue parka for protection from the cold, and picked up the string of pelts he wanted to sell in Prince Albert. He closed the door of his little house, tramped across the snowy field to the road and started walking east toward the highway, a stocky, middle-aged man, his diffidence showing in his posture. Small stones lay on top of the packed snow, where the reserve's grader had unearthed them. Snow is seldom deep in Saskatchewan, but it can pack like cement. Winds mould it into long narrow drifts shaped by tufts of grass, fence posts, and bumps in the ditches. There is not much along that road to stop the wind.

It is about a 170-kilometre drive to Prince Albert from the reserve. Leo could not afford a vehicle, but people frequently drive to Debden, just sixteen kilometres from the reserve, so it is not hard to get that far. Then, once at the main highway, it was easy to hitchhike to Prince Albert.

The gravel road out to the highway from the T-junction near his house runs past fields, farms, and clumps of bush. Outside the reserve, the farms are cleared and gently rolling. Although the soil is not terrific, a good farmer can make a living. That is not so on the reserve. There the land is rumpled by hills and gullies and the soil is

7

sand and gravel. The road there is level, cut through the narrow hills that cross it. The exposed innards of the mounds show barely an inch of topsoil on top of sand and gravel laid down eons ago by glacier-fed lakes and rivers. Some people raise cattle and grow a few crops, but the reserve is not capable of supporting all the people living on it, although the architects of the treaty said it would be. The land has never been farmed successfully, but the old people say a family can support itself with a garden, some chickens, and a cow. These days, few bother with even a garden. The gophers, rabbits, and deer snack elsewhere. Fruits and vegetables can be purchased at the store, and fresh meat in the form of deer, elk, and moose waits in the bush for skillful hunters. In the past, most people trapped or worked off the reserve as farm labourers or tree cutters for the pulp industry. Those jobs have nearly all disappeared as a result of technology and mechanization. Now welfare is the mainstay for many families.

The Green Lake Trail forms the main road through the reserve. Since the early fur trading days the trail connected the trading post at Green Lake, ninety-six kilometres north, with the Hudson's Bay Company's central station, Fort Carlton, ninety-six kilometres south, on the North Saskatchewan River, near Duck Lake. The trail was an offshoot of the Carlton Trail that joined Fort Garry, near present-day Winnipeg, Manitoba, and Fort Edmonton, Alberta. Many screeching Red River carts, the simple, efficient transportation used by the Métis, hauled trade goods to the western forts and returned with furs to Fort Garry. The sturdy carts were made entirely of wood and had no lubricants to quiet their squeals and screeches as they were pulled by the oxen or horses across the plains.

On the Green Lake Trail, on a ridge less than two kilometres from Leo's house, is a small graveyard where some of the traders and drovers are buried. Some say a white trader is buried there, with his fortune under his head, but no one on the reserve knows whether the story is true. If the white man wanted to be buried there, whatever is buried with him will stay there. No one will be allowed to disturb him.

The traders and drovers are gone, taking another source of income for the people of the reserve with them. However, the residents have never entirely stopped earning money by trapping furs. David and Albert LaChance still maintain traplines near Delaronde Lake, about twenty-five kilometres from their homes. Reduced incomes have always been supplemented by fishing for food. Whitefish Lake, on the reserve, still contains whitefish, pickerel, and trout. It is up to a hundred meters deep, and it curls around a point of land that juts out like an accusing finger at the revellers across the lake. The water is a deep blue, with shimmering pale green shoals and sandbars at intervals around the shore. The bottom drops off abruptly from the shoals, making them good fishing places. Miami Beach, as the locals sardonically call it, is a beautiful crescent of golden sand beach, but, unfortunately, it is strewn with garbage, not tourists, and no income results from its beauty.

The reserve is not much of a place to make a living, but it is beautiful. In the west, folds of misty blue hills stretch toward the sky. But when walking on a January afternoon at minus twenty-four degrees Celsius, one is more apt to be looking for a ride than admiring poetic hills. It is a long, frigid sixteen-kilometre walk along the road to Highway 55. Leo was not lucky that day. He had to walk almost to Debden before Chief John Keenatch and his daughter Patsy saw him and pulled over. Leo climbed into the back seat of their Buick Skylark.

Leo was apt to be talkative, joking and laughing, but not that day. John Keenatch found him unusually quiet. John and Leo had known each other all their lives: both men were born and grew up on the reserve. They had gone to school together and worked together. John had been one of the first chiefs elected, after hereditary chiefdoms were discontinued by the government. During his tenure, he negotiated the building of new homes for his people, and, in the process, created jobs. Like many of the Big River Reserve people, Leo appreciated what John had accomplished as chief. As for John, Leo was his friend and if he did not want to talk, that was fine.

The trip from Debden to Prince Albert takes about an hour. It is a fairly good two-lane highway all the way. The land is slightly rolling, mostly forested with pine, spruce, and fir, with large open areas where farms have been carved out of the forest. The towns of Debden, Canwood, and Shellbrook are situated along the way. The area is dotted with Cree Nation reserves: Ahtahkakoop, Mistawasis, and Big River. A fourth Cree community, Delaronde (Stoney Lake), probably should be a reserve but is not. For some reason, the government never surveyed it, although it promised it would. Nearer Prince Albert are the Sturgeon Lake Cree Nation Reserve and Wahpeton, a Dakota (Sioux) reserve. Many of the farms and forests they drove past that evening were familiar to Leo because he had worked over the years on so many of them, helping with the harvest or cutting posts.

Travelling east on Highway 3, toward the city, one sees the huge radar dish of the Prince Albert Satellite Station. Once it watched for Russian bombers as part of Canada's defense system. Now it tracks satellites and records their information.

The highway dips to cross the Shell River and the first of the acreages, modern homes with very large wooded lots, appear on either side of the highway. Then Highway 3 curves south and the lights of Prince Albert are visible ahead.

To approach Prince Albert from the north is to say goodbye to the forest on the banks of the North Saskatchewan River and say hello to the prairies on the south side. It is uncanny how the prairies, which every Canadian knows from picturesque calendars, roll to a stop on the south side of the river and the "true north strong and free" begins at the water's edge on the opposite side.

The Diefenbaker Bridge, four lanes wide, carries highways 2 and 3 into Prince Albert. As Chief Keenatch and his daughter approached the bridge, Leo LaChance asked Patsy to stop and let him out because he had to take a leak. He would walk the rest of the way he said. The Keenatches never saw him again.

Leo walked the five hundred metres across the bridge, clambered down the staircase onto the wide sidewalk of River Street, and headed east, toward Central Avenue and the heart of downtown. Across the street, on his left, was Reverend James Nisbet Memorial Park, a fifteen-metre-wide strip of grass, sloping down to the river, now covered in snow.

On his right were three old-fashioned stores with false fronts, rundown relics of a once-prosperous business district. In 1991, the first of these was a karate club. A narrow space between it and the next building was blocked by a sheet of corrugated iron to keep trespassers out. Scrap metal was piled behind the corrugated iron fence and covered with a makeshift roof. The second one-storey brick building housed two stores. The first store has a shabby yellow sign with faded black and white lettering hanging over the sidewalk, as it has for decades, announcing the presence of "Katz Bros. Hides Furs Metal." The second business was the Northern Pawn and Gun Shop. Each business has two display windows, one on either side of the recessed entrances. While Katz Bros. windows revealed odds and ends of scrap metal, water taps waiting to be useful one more time, and antlers suitable for hanging, the gun and pawn shop windows had little merchandise on display. Just the bare facts announced by a sign propped up between a table lamp and a cardboard box: GUNS AMMO LOANS. In the other window are Royal Canadian Air Force flags and old army surplus junk. No real treasures were to be found here, no items to lure casual browsers inside. They are two old stores, like aging twin dowagers waiting side by side. But while one is fortified by the standards of a lifetime, the other was twisted by bitterness and hate.

It was sometime after 5:30 P.M., 28 January, when Leo tried the door of the Katz Bros. fur and hide store and found it locked. He was disappointed. Arnold Katz was an old friend and Leo figured he would have paid him the few dollars the pelts were worth. Now what? It had been a long walk across the bridge and it was cold standing out on the street.

There is much speculation about Leo LaChance's next move. Some say that he likely went into the Northern Pawn and Gun Shop to get warm before he walked to a friend's place. Or maybe he saw something in the window he wanted to look at before he went on his way. Perhaps he hoped to sell or pawn his pelts there, although this seems unlikely because he left his pelts outside. Others say he thought Katz lived in the other half of the building, but that also seems unlikely. It is obviously a pawn shop, not a residence. His sister Roseanne wonders if he had pawned something earlier that he now wanted to retrieve, or if he owed the store owner money. He had received his welfare cheque earlier that day, yet when the police catalogued his belongings, he had only thirty cents in his pocket. Whatever the reason, Leo LaChance pushed the door open and stepped into the shop and headquarters of the leader of the Saskatchewan white supremacist movement.

The Northern Pawn and Gun Shop had a heavy old-fashioned door, nearly five centimetres thick, painted a ruddy brown, with a pane of glass from the top wooden panel to within a foot of the bottom of the door. It had a well-worn, curved door handle with a thumb latch. Above was a transom window. The shop inside was the same size as the fur and hide shop next door, but the layout was different. At Katz Bros., an antique counter along the left side divides the office space from the main area, which is furnished with a couch and a map of Canada, showing railway stops in towns that disappeared decades ago. The pawn and gun shop was seedy by comparison. An el-shaped counter ran the length of the store and along the back, separating the customers from the weapons displayed on the walls. There was a washroom and storage shelves built into the room along the inner wall. Boxes, tables, and a bit of counter ran along the left side, another table and boxes lined the back wall. Every flat surface was piled high with stacks of old sporting magazines, a Mandarin orange box of small pawned items, pieces of junk, old army helmets, ammunition belts. A full-length man's dark blue cape, with a Maltese cross on the left breast, hung from the ceiling. (Interestingly, an identical cape was displayed by the Order of the Solar Temple, which was discovered after the notorious mass murder of fifty-four cult members in Quebec and Switzerland in 1994.)

On the walls were flags hung haphazardly, army badges, pages from gun magazines, photographs, racks of guns, and a few other oddities. One was a sign that showed the silhouette of a black man inside a red circle, with a red slash through it like a traffic sign; apparently no blacks would be welcomed in this store. Some people claim they saw a Ku Klux Klan robe hanging from the wall. On the grubby open floor space in the rest of the tiny shop were the pawned items and other military and Nazi paraphernalia, helmets, badges, flags, canteens, parachute cases. The whole shop was no more than twenty square metres, and was crowded with piles of items for sale and by a Coca Cola machine next to the door, facing inwards. The door was hung with a red, yellow, and black Chilean flag, thumbtacked to the top of the window and falling just short of the bottom of the glass.

When Leo walked through the door, two other men were standing in front of the counter. Russ Yungwirth, a slight man with a black beard, was then a jail guard at the Prince Albert Correctional Centre. Gar Brownbridge, a stocky, clean shaven man, was a youth worker at the Prince Albert young offender facility. The two friends had met earlier that evening after work and had decided to visit Carney Nerland, who owned the gun shop. They drove together to River Street, and Brownbridge parked his car in front of the gun shop. When Yungwirth and Brownbridge entered the shop, Nerland was puttering behind the counter, as he often did. He was a heavy-set man, clean shaven, with thinning brown hair and features that were delicate for a person of his size. Most of his friends called him Milt. His Spanish-speaking wife disliked his first name, Carney, because it sounded like *carne*, the word for meat in Spanish.

Somehow, the gun deal Brownbridge was interested in was not discussed; instead, the three men talked about the Gulf War for almost two hours, drinking glasses of rye and cola as they talked. For most of the time, Brownbridge stood in front of the counter, talking to Nerland, who was leaning on the counter at the back of the store. Yungwirth rummaged through piles of pawned items on the west side of the store, occasionally taking part in the marathon discussion about the current war.

The door opened, causing the Chilean flag to billow slightly, and Leo LaChance stepped into the shop. It was obvious he was a Native; the LaChances all have handsome, sculpted faces, with high cheekbones and clear black eyes. Leo faced the three white men, Yungwirth, Brownbridge, and Carney Milton Nerland, a well-known white supremacist. The four men were the only witnesses to what happened next. Now, one is dead. One has disappeared. Two others want to put the whole experience behind them.

Later, Yungwirth and Brownbridge would claim that Leo was intoxicated when he entered the store. They said he wanted to sell a .303 rifle he did not have with him. They said Nerland fired two shots from the gun he had in his hand into the floor behind the counter. Then Leo turned to leave. They said they were shocked when a third shot rang out as the door was closing. They saw Nerland standing with the rifle in his hands, pointed at the door.

On River Street in the cold and the dark, Leo LaChance snatched up the furs he had left outside and started to walk along the sidewalk toward Central Avenue. Fifty metres down the street, he pitched face down in the snow.

CHAPTER THREE

The Place

No one saw the tragedy from across River Street. In winter, no one bothers to go to the downtown park. The only movement is the stiff, stilted sway of the tree branches in the frigid wind. By day, the riverbank is bluish-gray and white, broken only by the red of the willows along the far bank. At night, it is navy blue and black, relieved occasionally by headlights from vehicles along Highway 55 across the river from town.

Prince Albert's Reverend James Nisbet Memorial Park, which everyone calls simply "the riverbank," stretches for fifteen or twenty blocks in each direction from the downtown core at Central Avenue. It narrows to a few metres at the base of the Diefenbaker Bridge and broadens to as much as a few hundred metres at Charles Mair Ball Park where minor league softball diamonds are found. The iron railway bridge, a few metres west of Diefenbaker Bridge, has been there longer than any old-timer can remember. Before the turn of the century, the centre span used to turn to allow the wood burning steamboats and paddle wheelers to pass.

Children still try to beat trains across the bridge; if they cannot sprint fast enough, then they take refuge in the well of the turning mechanism, while the train rumbles overhead. Every year, a few souls give up in despair and throw themselves from one of the bridges. The fire department maintains a jet boat in an effort to reach them before they drown in the muddy, swift, roiling waters. Troy Cooper, the first police officer to reach the stricken Leo LaChance, once dove from the bank into the river after a suicidal jumper. It was April, just after the breakup. The ice flows hindered him but he reached her and got her to shore. But it was too late. She was dead from the shock and the cold.

As River Street follows the river downtown, the grassy bank slopes away from the sidewalk to the stone and cement wall that keeps the river from nibbling away at the bank. There used to be an iron railing along the wall, but that was torn out by the ice back in the 1940s. Since it is only a 1.5-metre fall to the soft mud in warm weather, the railing was never replaced. The river curves away from the foot of Central Avenue, the main street, as if to make room for bustling commerce, or to avoid the unhappiness of those who live there. This is where the very poor come to wander or "party," stealing surreptitious drinks from bags that hide bottles of "wine" concocted from Lysol disinfectant or Listerine mouthwash and tap water. This is the area where they live and, sometimes, it is where they die.

On some evenings in the warm summer the riverbank serves another purpose. Thousands lounge on the grassy slopes to watch with delight as Wes Stubbs, one-man dance band, marriage commissioner, justice of the peace, and former police chief, sets off the traditional holiday fireworks. The displays are held in semidarkness because Prince Albert is so far north that the sun does not set on Canada Day until after 10:00 P.M. The riverbank is also a sanctuary for the rebellious. Screened from sight by trees, teenagers are able to indulge the adult pursuits of drinking, sex, and drug deals.

The park shelters the Lund Wildlife Museum, a Red River cart bolted into permanent transit, a totem pole made by inmates of the federal penitentiary, and the inevitable Edwardian band shell. But in January, even the ravens and magpies avoid the place. The city's back alleys are theirs in winter; humans only make hasty trips to the dumpsters and then rush back indoors. Even stray dogs and cats find somewhere out of the cold. In January there can be a wicked wind from the river and temperatures fall beyond mercy into the minus thirty and forty degrees Celsius range. Huge ravens clutch branches of riverbank trees and fluff their feathers into shaggy robes against the wind. They know there is nothing to eat along River Street, so they soar again to the top of the fifteen-storey Marquis Towers apartment building and survey the downtown area for food to peck at and argue over.

One hundred years ago, River Street was the major business district. Now it is just another thoroughfare from east to west with very few shops skirting the downtown shopping area. One hundred years ago, there was no contoured lawn smoothly joining the road and the river, no paved pathways, no museums, no pawn shops, no bridges spanning the fast moving, murky river. But River Street was special — the centre of town, a hive of activity. Pollution was not an issue in pioneering days, and the riverbank was a place to dump refuse. The shaggy grass and weeds held many tidbits for the scavenging ravens who competed with the roaming dog packs for the good stuff.

One hundred years ago there was a popcorn vendor who wore a bowler hat that looked like a fat raven's belly. He had a big, glass-domed pushcart that sent waves of wonderful smells into the air and drew the attention of birds and promenaders alike. The humans were sloppy and spilled. The ravens meticulously cleaned up after them as soon as they were gone. There once was a potato chip truck too, fifty years ago. Little children were sure to spill fat fries from the greasy little paper cones, and ravens could be counted on to be there, shouldering aside the cocky gulls, to grab and gulp. In the summer of 1899, there was a parade along River Street, with a dozen elephants and hundreds of spectators. The Walter L. Main Circus left a banquet on the ground. The ravens liked the circus.

By sitting where the totem pole is now, or on the benches around the band shell, facing away from the river, one could see River Street from Central Avenue — to the very place where Leo LaChance was shot.

Prince Albert was founded in 1866, a full fifteen years before most western towns. By the early 1880s, there were buildings and businesses strung out for eight kilometres along River Street. There were seven general stores and two hardware and novelty stores. There were furniture emporiums, shoe stores, residences, businesses, law offices. There were doctors, dentists, and druggists in town. There was a planing mill, a door and sash business, bakeries, and banks. Townfolk and farmers, fur trappers and traders, prospectors and politicians — all made their way along the rutted, muddy thoroughfare that was River Street, famed for its potholes but heralded as the main street of a city that was going places, the city that would be the biggest and most famous in all the west.

Prince Albert had all the ingredients for success and it showed on River Street: the enterprise, the people, the enthusiasm, the resources, the hunting, fishing, and trapping, the river itself. There was even gold in the mighty North Saskatchewan River.

Everyone expected the mainline of the Canadian Pacific Railway to come soon to Prince Albert and for the station to be built on River Street. That railway would make Prince Albert a city to be reckoned with, a leader in every respect, a giant of trade and commerce. The railway would make Prince Albert The City. None other would compare. The future was glorious and speculation was rife.

Instead, the Canadian Pacific Railway main line was suddenly rerouted in 1881 and it put Pile of Bones, renamed Regina, on the map as Queen City instead. That was a blow, but there were other railways negotiating for access to Prince Albert. Maybe the Manitoba and Northwestern Railway, already to Yorkton, or maybe the Hudson's Bay Railway, still in the dream stage, would reach Prince Albert soon. Sure enough, each year railway after railway announced its plans to reach Prince Albert and profit by shipping grain east and settlers and fancy goods west. Each year, however, their plans were cancelled. The city was founded without railways (unlike most prairie cities, which sprang up along the tracks) and it would prosper until the branch lines finally found their way north in 1890 to join Prince Albert with the towns the railways had created. The dream of Prince Albert as the premier city of the west never dimmed. That faith was rather severely tested on occasion, and at times it gave rise to some rather tenuous schemes. Local promoters once saw Prince Albert as a jumping-off spot for Yukon gold rush hopefuls. They hoped would-be millionaires would buy their outfits in Prince Albert and travel north by water. Unfortunately, the trek from Prince Albert to Dawson City was too long and too dangerous. The prospectors took no chances and bought their gear elsewhere. Still, the citizens' faith remained firm and, unlike so many other prairie outposts of the nineteenth century, the town did not fade away after its plans were dashed.

Prince Albert is situated in a setting almost identical to Grand Valley, Manitoba, another would-be boom town. Both had a hill at their backs. Both occupied a broad, flat river plain of rich farmland which extended for kilometres along a broad, navigable river. Both expected the railroads to choose their site for a terminus and both were disappointed. But in 1994, Prince Albert is a bustling city of more than thirty-five thousand, while Grand Valley has disappeared. There is not even a depression in the ground to indicate a town once thrived there.

The North Saskatchewan River was always Prince Albert's raison d'être. It brought the Métis families who farmed there years before the first white settlers founded the fledgling town in 1866. Current maps of the area still show the distinctive French Canadian strip farms, long and narrow, each with its own access to the river, for drinking water and transportation, set in neat angled rows west and north of the present city. Métis farm lots persisted through history, even though the government imposed the rigid square-mile townships on the virgin prairie. People had faith in the land. Here they could prosper and build their dreams.

The prairies have an unusual beauty, a vastness of land and sky that is stunning. Once settlers had seen it from their own doorsteps, it became hard to give up their dreams. The setbacks, economic disasters, and the phenomenal cold were only hurdles, not roadblocks, in their determination to succeed.

Meanwhile, there was the river and River Street. There had been trappers and traders on that thoroughfare for hundreds of years, before railways were conceived, and there will be trappers and traders outfitting and selling and meeting in Prince Albert for years to come. River Street lost its prominence in the twentieth century, but it is still there, serving as a vital artery for the better-off and remaining the heart of town for the poor. Here are the pawn shops, the fur and scrap metal buyers, the Share A Meal and Food Bank, and the businesses that have thrived there for decades. The National Hotel, constructed in 1906, stands across from the Prince Albert Hardware store, which was originally built as a bank in 1905. After the bank moved, the building was briefly used as a North West Mounted Police barracks. Bars were placed on the bathroom window after a prisoner escaped and ran naked down River Street. Steve Luciuk turned the bank building into the hardware store in the 1950s and also began the Empire Grocery next door. The Empire building stands empty now but Luciuk's daughter, Marlene, and her husband, Ron LaFaver, still operate the hardware store.

Almer's Music Store, at 61 River Street West, traces its roots to Syria. Frank Almer Sr. came to this country at the turn of the century and operated a travelling pedlar business in the northwest for years, finally settling in Prince Albert. He founded his general store on River Street in 1929, now Almer's Music Store. Frank Sr. was rumoured to be the seventh son of a seventh son and he and his wife, Nancy, had seven children. He had a psychic's ability to find things for people and the seventh son story persists even though his family now discounts it.

United Office Machines, on the corner of Central Avenue and River Street, was also built in 1905. Steve Paslowski started a one-man business there in 1946 and is still president and general manager with nineteen staff members. He was only twenty-four years old then, the same age Carney Nerland was in his first year of business. Now seventy three, Paslowski is still at his desk every day, supervising nineteen staff members.

Davidner's clothing, around the corner, caters to people who work outdoors on rough and dirty jobs. It was established in 1932 and expanded to become a western wear centre.

And then there are the here-for-awhile-and-quickly-gone businesses such as the Prince Albert Northern Pawn and Gun Shop.

CHAPTER FOUR

The Night

When Leo LaChance fell face down in the snow, he instinctively turned his head. He passed out, crumpled on the snowy sidewalk of a dark and nearly deserted street. It was very cold. A passerby hurried out of the darkness, bent over Leo, then quickly walked toward the Northern Pawn and Gun Shop. Leo needed help urgently, that was clear.

Abruptly, Leo regained consciousness. What was happening to him? He was aware now of the terrible pain. It was growing, moving, and turning in his chest like a caged animal. What the hell was it? Those white guys must have shot him! When? Why?

He had to get up and get out of there. Somebody was coming toward him. He could not focus on the man's face. Who was it? Oh — Maurice Morin! "My brother. My brother," Leo cried out in Cree. Morin was a cousin, a friend, one of his own. Somebody to help him. But Morin was pushing him back down. Telling him to lie still.

"Fuck you!"

Oh the pain! The pain was trying to tear its way out of his chest. He sank back in the snow. A third Good Samaritan, Donald Blunden, produced a blanket and Morin covered Leo gently. Another was placed under his head. He rested for a few seconds. The pain raged, it burned, it clawed. He could not get his breath. He could not talk.

It was dark. The street light was across the street, farther down. There was another stranger standing over him now. He was bending down, touching Leo's sleeve. What could he want? Was he going to finish the job? Leo did not know this man. When would his buddy Morin take him home? The white man who had just arrived was speaking to Leo. What was he saying? He had called the police. An ambulance was coming, he said. The pain was so strong. Everything went black.

The first man on the scene after Leo fell was Kim Koroll, a draftsman with the city engineering department. He had been driving west along River Street when he noticed Leo walking toward him. He saw him pitch face first into the snow. He quickly braked, parked his vehicle, and hurried across River Street.

LaChance was unconscious. Since there was no sign of a wound or blood, there was no way for a nonprofessional to tell what was wrong. But clearly LaChance needed help. Koroll looked around. There were lights on in the Northern Pawn and Gun Shop. He hurried over and entered the store. Three men were standing there. He said he believed that the man behind the counter had a beard. Koroll does not remember quite how he put it, but he knows he made it clear he wanted to use the telephone to call 911. "No," he was told. "There is no phone." Koroll hurried out to search for a telephone. He cut through a back alley and jumped a fence alongside the A & W where he finally found one, two blocks from where Leo lay in the snow.

The 911 call was clocked at 6:39 P.M. The ambulance was nearby and arrived within three minutes. Paramedics Pat Bellisle and Rob Ferland knelt down beside the fallen LaChance and began their standard ABC procedures: airway, breathing, and circulation checks. They knew the man was in trouble, but they did not yet know why. There was no blood or sign of seizure, just a semiconscious man lying on his side in the snow. And there was a cold wind off the river.

Leo was not doing well on the ABC tests. He was having difficulty breathing and his pulse was not good. He was shivering with the cold. Bellisle decided the street was no place to remove the injured man's coat and begin a further examination. The paramedics put their arms under his shoulders and legs and gently lifted him onto a stretcher. At the same time, they questioned the witnesses for any clues they might have about Leo's condition. Morin had already left. Only the two white men remained and they could only repeat that they had seen him fall and had stopped and tried to help him. They did not know anything further. To complicate matters, Leo LaChance had identified himself to the paramedics as Leo Roberts, a name he sometimes used for reasons of his own.

Inside the ambulance Pat Bellisle removed Leo's jacket and began searching for clues as to why this man had keeled over in the street. In ninety seconds, Bellisle pulled off the left sleeve of Leo's jacket and had his answer. This was not another Saturday night "special," someone too drunk to talk. This man's left arm was broken and there was blood on his arm and his rib cage. He had been either shot or stabbed. It seemed impossible to Bellisle that Leo had been shot. Hardly anyone gets shot in Prince Albert. Victims get stabbed or beaten. But LaChance was mumbling "gun shot" or was it "gun shop"? Whatever it was, the police needed to be told immediately.

The ambulance driver, Rob Ferland, was just pulling away from the curb. He stopped suddenly and signalled the police cruiser behind him to pull up alongside. He did not want to use the radio, monitored by everyone with a police scanner. "This guy has been either shot or stabbed," Ferland told the two police officers. Constable Ian Reiman radioed a coded message to the police station. The ambulance pulled away and the cruiser fell in place behind it. Pat Bellisle never paused in his examination of LaChance. Leo's pulse dropped from 120 to 112 in the three minutes it took to get from the 100 block on River Street West to the Holy Family Hospital.

Bellisle staunched the bleeding and started the oxygen. He cut away LaChance's sweater and shirt and saw the bullet wound in LaChance's left side. He could not see an exit wound. Leo's left arm, he saw, was obviously broken, swollen, and distorted. In such a short distance, there was no time to start an intravenous. That would be ready and waiting at the hospital. The paramedic was aware of the need to preserve evidence and to take a dying statement if necessary, but there was a problem. Leo LaChance was weak and drifting in and out of consciousness. It was impossible to make out his words, or even to tell if they were English or Cree.

Four minutes after he was loaded into the ambulance, LaChance was in the emergency ward of the hospital. His pulse was weak and his breathing shallow. His blood pressure was dropping into the critical range. He was clearly in pain and in shock. He responded to voices by opening his eyes, but he still could not make people understand what he was trying to say.

What Carney Milton Nerland was saying was being understood well enough. "If I shot that Indian, I'm fucked. My business is fucked," he told Russ Yungwirth and Gar Brownbridge.

Brownbridge could not believe what he had just seen. As the door clicked shut behind LaChance he heard a shot fired. Looking at Nerland, he saw that the gun shop owner was standing facing the door, lowering his M-56 semiautomatic rifle. "You silly bugger! You could have hit my car!" Brownbridge snapped at him and went to the window to look across the sidewalk at his vehicle, parked in front of the door. He did not see LaChance and he did not look for him.

As soon as the shooting occurred, Nerland hastily began to close up shop. Brownbridge and Yungwirth started for the door, but Nerland told them to stand still while he set his burglar alarm. Then, carrying three weapons, he followed the two men to the car and sat in the front seat. Brownbridge's car was facing east. To drive that way meant passing the spot where LaChance had fallen. The three men claimed they saw nothing. Brownbridge "pulled a U-ball" and drove in the opposite direction, to the Canadian Tire store at the south end of the city. When another police car turned onto River Street, four minutes after the 911 call was received, the parking lane was empty in front of Nerland's store. The three men had already left.

Once they arrived at the Canadian Tire store, Brownbridge went in alone to get some cash on his credit card. When he returned to the car, he asked Nerland if he wanted to join them at Brownbridge's home to watch some videos. Nerland said no. He wanted a ride back to his car that was parked behind the gun shop on River Street.

When they returned to the store, Yungwirth peered up the street in the direction LaChance had gone. If anything had happened, surely there would be police, roadblocks, a crowd. He saw nothing. Yungwirth did not guess that Leo LaChance had already been taken to hospital where he was fighting for his life.

CHAPTER FIVE

The Next Day

29 January 1991

Big River Reserve

David LaChance was sitting at his kitchen table, drinking a mug of tea and listening to Saskatchewan's morning news on CBC radio. "Prince Albert police report a man died early this morning in a Saskatoon hospital after being shot Monday evening on River Street in Prince Albert. Police are not releasing the name of the victim, pending notification of next of kin. There have not been any arrests and police are still investigating."

David went cold. How did he know it was Leo? He was not even sure if his brother had gone to Prince Albert, but he got up, put on his jacket and boots, and went across the road to Leo's house. There was no light. With a sinking heart, he went in the back door. There was a note propped up on the kitchen table. "Gone to Prince Albert. Be back tomorrow. Leo."

David left and hurried down the hill to his gas station and pool hall where he telephoned the Big River RCMP. "This is David LaChance." The RCMP there know David as a good man and a friend. They had been trying to reach him, they said. A special constable would leave for David's home immediately.

"I'll tell you what kind of man David LaChance is. If he came to my door right now and asked for a thousand dollars, I'd give it to him," says a Big River business owner. David is seen as a leader by many people, on the reserve and off. The Native community has a great deal of respect for him. He is honest and fair. Over sixty, he has the strong, wiry physique of a man who has earned his living through hard, physical work in the outdoors — on farms, planting, harvesting, and driving teams of plow horses, clearing bush, picking rocks, and, for many years, building roads for a firm just outside of Big River, a town forty kilometres northeast of the reserve. That job in the 1950s, and several years working for a farmer in Alberta, allowed him to save enough money to buy his own team of horses and a caboose which he used to provide the first "school bus" service on the reserve.

When a white man brought school buses to the reserve, David drove for him for years until he had enough money to buy his own buses. He still owns two school vehicles that he and his children, Leroy and Brenda, drive. However, after Leo died, he sold the pool hall and gas station across from his home. The number of people who would wake him in the middle of the night looking for gas and refusing to believe the station was closed discouraged him as much as anything. He has been a trapper all his life, with a cabin and a trapline north of the reserve near Prince Albert National Park at Delaronde Lake.

David has been a band councillor for sixteen years, one of a twelve-man council that is elected every four years and meets regularly to advise the band chief. Band councils are not like city councils where a vote on every matter large and small is taken. The bands operate in traditional Indian ways. Each matter is discussed until a consensus is reached.

David is most often seen wearing the uniform of the outdoorsman: work pants with suspenders, a workshirt, work boots, and a ball cap. He is not a tall man and he is spare. His close-cropped hair is gray and his bronzed face is a map of a lifetime of laughter and tragedy.

David and Leo LaChance were half-brothers. He and Leo had

the same black eyes, high cheekbones, and bronze skin of the Cree. Their skin is the glowing bronze colour people spend millions trying to achieve. As the youth of today say, "It is a suntan to die for." And, apparently, it is what Leo LaChance did die for: bronzed skin, singling him out as an Indian.

The first and lasting impression David gives is of a quiet dignity and determination. In some ways, David is the embodiment of the Cree people. He has suffered and will continue to suffer. When required to do so, he steps firmly into the spotlight of national media scrutiny. He is not self-conscious. He is not demanding. There is no arrogance. There is only a quiet determination to do, step by step, whatever is necessary to understand why Leo, his brother, a Cree man, was shot to death by a white man, seemingly for no reason. He summed it up once by saying, "I want to know the truth about what happened that night." He has no political or financial base to support him. His quest will not cease until he is satisfied he has learned the truth.

On Big River Reserve is divided, north and south, into Roman Catholic and Anglican communities because schooling was provided by the Anglicans in the north and by Roman Catholics in the south. It was not until the 1970s that the reserve was united into one school. People still tend to know friends and relatives in their own area, however, and it is not unusual for families in one area not to have heard of families in the other.

The reserve is a large irregular block shaped like the state of California. It is twenty-nine kilometres long and ten kilometres wide at its widest point. A small section containing the village of Victoire, a church, and the store is located south of the main reserve. Some of the land around Victoire used to be owned by the band but was sold years ago, and is now farm land separating the village from the main reserve.

Big River Reserve is essentially flat, but there are hills and ridges rising among the poplars. It is dotted by small lakes in a glacier-made chain, leading north. Dirt roads crisscross the reserve, leading to clusters of houses dotted all over the land. From the main dirt road, the reserve looks deserted, yet homes for nearly eighteen hundred people are tucked away on the myriad side roads.

The band office is a modern structure, built on a ridge overlooking Whitefish Lake. Below the road leading to the office is an alluring strip of sandy lake shore. Farther on is an attractive school built in 1975/76, offering elementary classes for four hundred students. The elders take part in the programming, helping the children to know and appreciate their culture. Many of the teachers speak Cree, and classes are taught in Cree and English.

Along the road is a large field where the sun dances are held. Centre poles and pavilions of earlier sun dance rituals still stand as though waiting to be dressed again in fresh ceremonial branches. A new tree is cut and dragged to the field for each dance. It is anchored in a pit and stripped of all the limbs except for a crown of trimmed branches that looks like a crow's nest. It is on this platform that special religious supplications are made. Dancers circle the tree during the celebrations. The dance area is circled by pavilions made of poles and branches that shelter and shade the observers and the singers.

The RCMP know their way through the reserve and can easily find the house they are looking for, though none are marked with street addresses or names. Too often, their missions on the reserve are to bring bad news to one family or another. The police officer who came to see David the morning his brother Leo died was no stranger. He told David what little was known at that point: Leo had been in a gun shop next to Katz Bros. Furs in Prince Albert. He had been shot and managed to walk a few metres up River Street toward town before he collapsed. He was taken to Royal University Hospital in Saskatoon for emergency surgery. He died on the operating table at approximately fifty-five minutes after midnight, January 29. The Prince Albert City Police were investigating the killing.

This was not the first death. This was not the second. This was the third of David's brothers and sisters to die violently and without explanation. And these were not the only family tragedies in recent years.

Three kilometres down the main road past Leo's former house is the Whitefish Mission of the Roman Catholic church. Two nuns, Sisters of the Presentation of Mary, live in a small older home on the shores of one of the many nameless small lakes on the reserve. Their door is always open to those who need to talk, and they offer Sunday School, Bible studies, prayer group leadership, and even the Rosary spoken over the telephone. Often they work in concert with Native elders, spiritual leaders, and Protestant missions. Their living room-cum-office looks across a field to the church. People find comfort there, talking about their grief.

Twice in seventeen months the sisters have helped David and Madeline prepare funerals for their sons. Kelvin was seventeen when he died in a car crash on the reserve in October 1992. Leon David at age twenty-three would die in February 1994. He was found frozen to death on the reserve a week after he had disappeared. Both young men were victims of alcohol.

Just a few months before Kelvin died, Chief John Keenatch, the old friend of Leo's who had driven him to Prince Albert the night he was shot, and his wife, Marguerite, died in a car accident on the reserve when a drunk driver crashed his into them. But then, death frequently stalks the reserves. The service for the dead reads, "In life, we are in the midst of death. . . ." It is seldom truer than on a reserve. It used to be disease that stole the young. Now it is alcohol.

In Prince Albert, Lysol cans, Listerine bottles, and hairspray containers litter the alleyways behind the stores on Central Avenue near the river, the riverside park, and under the bridges and viaducts. The price of Lysol has risen steadily over the years, but it is easily available. Occasionally, it seems to police, some stores stock more cases of Lysol than the entire city would require, no matter how sanitation-minded it might become. The denizens of the park can quote Lysol prices for every store in the area and know where to get it at the lowest price and with the least hassle — some places, like the Co-op, do not hand it over easily.

The spray can is emptied of the liquid Lysol, which is drunk straight or mixed with water. The new one with the blue label is not nearly as good as the old one with the green label, they say.

Even the veteran street people fear the latest cheap drink: Alberto VO-5 hairspray. They urge their friends not to touch it. "That stuff will kill you for sure," they say. But some drink it anyway. "You don't get drunk, you get high on that stuff," a former user said. He drank it for awhile before checking himself into a rehabilitation centre. He was extremely ill for two weeks but he was cured once and for all. That and seeing friend after friend die from drinking the stuff. Half a dozen of Leo's friends have died in the past three years, most of them from imbibing Lysol or hairspray.

In the old days, lemon extract was the drink of choice. Then Black Magic (vanilla extract) took away the pain. These were followed by hair lotion, mouthwash, Lysol, and now hairspray. If it has alcohol in it and is cheap, then it becomes an inexpensive transport from reality. Anyone who has a little money buys and shares. Everyone is equal on the street. Former street people will tell you that it is those who live on the streets and drink under the bridges and in the parks who truly love other people, not the ministers or social workers.

Leo enjoyed Prince Albert's street life. A friend had built a little shack of cardboard and plastic sheeting in the pines across the river. There was a frying pan and a coffee pot and a sleeping bag. In bad weather, it was a cozy, friendly spot to drink. Leo liked camping out in the bush at the far west end of the riverbank park too. He loved to tease his friends and make them laugh. They still chuckle at the memories and say, "That Leo. He was a crazy guy. He was always doing something to make you laugh."

His sister, Roseanne, wakes in the night and tries to cope with the pain. "It really hurts. It bothers me so much he died that way: helpless and afraid. Why?"

CHAPTER SIX

The Family

Leo LaChance was born in December 1943, in the family's log cabin on the Big River Indian Reserve. He was the fifth child of Agnes LaChance to live to adulthood. Agnes later told her surviving daughter, Roseanne, that she lost count after twenty-one miscarriages, stillbirths, and babies who lived only a few hours or days.

Roseanne is younger than Leo but she remembers the birth of one of her younger siblings. She looked out the window and saw her mother bent over a horizontal pole that had been rigged up for her to hang onto during her labour. Roseanne saw the newborn on the ground at her mother's feet. She also remembers seeing the baby in a hammock in the log cabin but its tiny head was misshapen and it did not live long. Roseanne believes malnutrition may explain why her mother lost so many babies. She had no breast milk to feed them because she had so little to eat.

Leo was one of the survivors, along with Albert, born in 1928, Josephine, born in 1929, David in 1933, and Samarie in 1941. The older three children were the sons and daughter of David LaChance Sr. Samarie and Leo, and later Roseanne and Virginia, were the children of Agnes's second marriage to Dick LaChance. All of the LaChance children were born at home and baptised on the Big River Reserve at the Sacred Heart Roman Catholic mission church.

The Big River Reserve is a traditional one. During World War II the elders obeyed the letter of the treaty that said Indians had agreed not to take up arms again and the king would protect the people. No young man from the Big River Reserve was allowed to break that treaty by joining the armed forces during World War II, even though nearby reserves interpreted the treaty differently. The only evidence of the war on the reserve was the rationing of tea, sugar, meat, butter, and fuel. For once the Indians were better-off than the whites. Indians could supplement the rations by hunting and fishing year round. Leo was only two years old when peace was declared.

Leo spent his babyhood in his hammock of blanket and rope in the cabin or in his moss bag, warm and comforting, hanging from a branch of a tree outside. He listened to the soughing of the wind in the pines and firs and the raspy rustle of the budding poplars. The cool breeze put him to sleep and played with him when he awoke, twisting his moss bag so the world of trees, lake, and meadow became a kaleidoscope to his infant eyes. Tiny ears listened to the songs of chickadees, robins, and the ever-mournful whistle of the white-throated sparrows. He heard the laughter and chatter of his brothers and sister playing or working below. His mother, Agnes, worked nearby chopping firewood or tanning hides or drying meat and fish for the winter. Work was endless for everyone. If they did not constantly work hard, they starved to death. It was that kind of simple life.

First thing in the morning Dick LaChance and his sons, including Leo when he was old enough, checked the snares for rabbits and picked fresh Labrador tea, the leaves of an evergreen that make a fragrant brew. His mother drew water from the river, started the fire in the wood stove for breakfast, and made bannock from lard, flour, baking powder, salt, and water. Baked in a pan, it tastes much like the baking powder biscuits or scones of other countries.

When Leo was growing up, the Big River Reserve was like another country. No one could enter or leave without the permission of the Indian agent and the chief, both chosen by the government of Canada on behalf of the king. Money did not change hands except on Treaty Day when the chief was entitled to ten dollars (to be subtracted from his annual salary of twenty-five dollars) and everyone else was entitled to a payment of five dollars for signing away the land now owned by the Dominion of Canada. Anything else was paid for in chits that could be traded for supplies. Only those who were too old to work were given food: bacon, flour, tea, and a bit of sugar once every two weeks.

The men hunted deer, bear, and moose and trapped beaver, muskrat, fox, weasels, fishers, wolverines, lynx, and wolves. The women snared rabbits and squirrels and fished in the lakes and streams for their family's endless need for food. The children helped, too, and sometimes caught gophers by pouring water into their dens. The gophers could be eaten and the tails sold for a small bounty. Rabbits were another source of supply and cash. Agnes dried and finished the rabbit skins, and the children used them as socks in the winter. In later years they were able to sell rabbit skins at the store for a nickel each.

Dick LaChance was a strong believer in the value of hard work. It was his measuring stick for those he approved of and those he did not. Leo never quite measured up. Still, Leo was a happy little boy who adored his mother and trotted around after the other children, laughing and playing. Soon he was old enough to follow his brothers down the buffalo trail through the bush to the main road on the six-kilometre trek to school each day. The LaChance children attended the one-room school operated by Father Paquette and nuns from the Order of The Daughters of Providence.

The meadow where the LaChance home was built is beautiful, calm and quiet in human terms, but alive with the busy lives of the insects and animals that live there too: moles, chipmunks, squirrels, rabbits, skunks, mice, weasels, raccoons, moose, elk, deer, ladybugs, ants, mosquitoes, spiders, flies, and the million kinds of tiny insects only entomologists have names for. The birds on the hop in the poplars produce a constant background music, punctuated by the cries of Mallard ducks flying to and from the lakes and sloughs, as well as the everpresent ravens, magpies, and gulls making their daily station calls in search of feeding spots. The lake laps at the shore not three hundred metres from where the LaChance house stood. The slap and hiss of the waves on the sand and rock soothed the young Leo LaChance.

There was a bare living to be made in the 1940s, as long as everyone worked hard. But after the war it was possible to get farm work off the reserve. At last the people from the reserve were allowed more freedom to leave it and to seek work as labourers on farms in Saskatchewan and Alberta or to work in the bush cutting logs or fence posts. These jobs and trapping brought in cash.

Eventually, in the 1950s, mothers began to receive the Family Allowance of six dollars per child from the Canadian government. Although there were now means of obtaining a little money to improve their life-style, it was nothing compared to the opportunities available to people off the reserve. Reserve life remained a stand-still life-style in a move-ahead country that was enjoying a postwar economic boom.

Some reserves, like nearby Chitek Lake, a Saulteaux reserve, would not allow any dealings with whites, at least not until the elders were all gone. The Chitek Lake band did not sign the treaty until November 1950, seventy-five years after everyone else.

But for most bands, reserve life had been accepted when the whiteman moved west and the old way of life disappeared. The white nation was surging ahead with endless opportunities. The Indian nations were waiting for whatever chances they would be allowed. Reserve life was accepted for the most part and made better anyway it could be through the efforts of the people. This was the Cree nation: patient, enterprising, and wanting to succeed. Its time would come again.

Dick LaChance built the family's log house from wood on the property, just as two of his sons, Leo and David, built a similar log cabin in the same meadow forty-five years later. In the early days, when a man had the walls of a cabin up, he could apply to the Indian agent for a grant of seventy-five dollars for roofing, windows, and a door.

Living on the reserve in those days was like living on an island in the middle of nowhere. By law, Indians could not leave without a reason and a permit. Whether the reason was considered good enough depended on what the Indian agent thought at the time, not on what the Indian applicant had decided was necessary. There was little money, no radio, and no television. The outside world was a foreign place to the members of the Big River band. The only whites there were the Indian agent, the nuns and priests, some teachers, and the occasional nurse, doctor, or government official. Visitors from other reserves were welcome indeed, for they brought news.

Yet today's grandmothers and great-grandmothers remember the war years on the reserve as happy times. Everyone was busy with their tasks. The children attended school and helped at home fetching water and gathering berries, duck eggs, or moss or helping with the younger children. True, there were no toys and no extra food; the LaChance children were hopeful when they hung stockings on the foot of their beds on Christmas Eve but when they awoke, the stockings were always empty. Yet there were always things to do: playing soccer or hockey or sliding down the ridge toward Keg Lake. Once Leo's brother David made himself a pair of skis. There were friends to run and play with and to share secrets. Leo was in the thick of it. Even then, his easy-going nature won him friends. He could get along with anyone.

Education was much the same across Canada in 1949, the year Leo was old enough to start school. Boys wore shirts and trousers; girls wore dresses; nuns wore long, full habits. There was no talking, no gum chewing, and no running inside. The daily round consisted of subjects, predicates, common denominators, explorers, Dick and Jane, My Speller, recess, and Neilsen maps of the world. The British Empire was pink and portraits of the king and queen smiled faintly at the children from above the teacher's desk.

No Cree was spoken at the Roman Catholic mission school on the Big River Reserve. No Ukrainian, French, Dutch, Walloon, or Polish was spoken in Prince Albert schools. The difference was that immigrants had a limitless future in Canada in 1949. The Indians had no future at all. Canadians could go anywhere, try anything. Leo's family needed permission to set foot off the reserve, to chop wood, to haul water, to go to the store, to see the doctor, or to change their property in any way. Whites could be doctors or bricklayers or mathematicians or storekeepers or anything they fancied being. Leo's future was either staying on the reserve where there was little work, or leaving to look for farm or forest industry labour jobs. School was fine, but for Indians it did not lead anywhere. An Indian was isolated on the reserve and ignorant of the larger world, so there was no motivation to master the white man's learning to take him places he did not know or care about. From Leo's point of view, there was little more off the reserve than there was on it. There was no particular reason to learn about buses and streetcars, Africans and antiquities. Who ever expected to see such exotic things?

Leo liked school well enough but he did not like the strict discipline meted out by the nuns. He would rather fish or go hunting or swimming. Because the Daughters of Providence came to the reserve to teach in 1942, Leo did not have to attend the residential school at Duck Lake as Albert and David did for part of their schooling. Like every Canadian child, he learned that Indians lived in tipis, wore furs, and used every part of the buffalo, even though he personally had never seen a buffalo. Leo's classmates wrote a history about Indian life on the reserve, yet it was written entirely in the third person. It was as though they were writing about beings they had never seen rather than about themselves, their people, their own homes and families. Leo learned about the explorers, La Vérendrye, Radisson, and Groseilliers (Radishes and Gooseberries as they were coyly nicknamed by Canadian teachers, to aid the memory). He did not learn about the impact these men had on his own life and on hundreds of years of Cree history. In fact, he did not learn Cree history at all. None of the children did. The government believed it was unimportant and would only hinder the Indians' assimilation. Assimilation was the goal in 1949. The government seemed to think that if Indians could just be made to look, act, and think like whites, then maybe something could be done with them.

Leo did not care if anyone wanted him to assimilate or not. He was just a happy-go-lucky child, playing with his friends and his brothers. Leo started at the Catholic school on the reserve and there he remained until grade six or seven, when his parents, in the late 1950s, got permission to go to Alberta to work in the sugar beet fields. Leo went with them, and that ended his formal education.

CHAPTER SEVEN

The Sweet Grass Trail

Leo's sister Roseanne looked forward to summers in the sugar beet fields. She was ready to go long before the old buses arrived to gather workers from the reserves and transport them to the farms near Taber, Alberta. It was an opportunity to do something different and be somewhere else for awhile. It was exciting.

But the work was hard. Endless rows of beets were weeded by backbreaking hoeing. A row of beets could be almost one kilometre long, a long kilometre for a child.

Sugar beets look like oversized yellowish-white carrots. In those days, the growing plants were thinned by hand – one every twenty-five centimetres. They had to be hoed free of weeds two or three times before the tops were tied and the beets harvested by machine. If the first hoeing was done well, then second and third hoeings were much easier and faster and more money could be earned. The farm hands were paid by the acre. Some farmers paid a worker the same as he or she would earn in town in a twelve-hour day. Others were not so generous. Some kept good, clean fields. Others had dirty fields that were a nightmare to weed and a poor prospect for the hapless worker hoping to earn much money.

Today machines plant seeds every eighteen centimetres and the fields are chemically treated to discourage weeds. But in the 1940s, when the Japanese internees were brought to Taber to work the fields, it was the same backbreaking hand work the Indians later faced. The Japanese worked hard to get out of the fields. Now many of them and their children own the sugar beet and potato farms in southern Alberta. In the late 1940s and early 1950s, after the war, the Dutch refugees and then the Hungarians fleeing the 1956 revolution took over the field work. They too struggled to get out on their own. Then came the Indians to hoe the fields and harvest the potatoes by hand. For the most part, they had nowhere to struggle to. They were eventually replaced by modern machinery that eliminated thinning and hoeing, although some second-generation Indians still work in the Taber fields for a few weeks each year.

The families lived in cabins on the farms and everyone did whatever jobs were available, the boys eventually graduating to driving tractors or trucks for the farmers. There were potato fields to harvest as well as general farm work for everyone to do.

For the First Nations people, the poverty, the rationing, and the rules were accepted as the way things were. There was no talk of rebellion against the system. Instead, the chiefs continued to petition the government and to win whatever changes they could, however small, for the betterment of their people. The Department of Indian Affairs continued to be fantastically slow at making changes but the First Nations people never gave up. When the people moved to the reserves in the 1870s, the elders predicted that it would take seven generations "to bring the buffalo back," before the people again achieved freedom, self-government, and pride in themselves as a nation. Leo and Roseanne LaChance were of the fifth generation.

By the time Leo was twenty-five, Indians were allowed leave the reserves if they wished and work wherever they could find employment.

But their world was hardly a paradise. With little to do and less to hope and strive for, many people began to drink to forget, as their unhappy counterparts around the world have done for centuries. The beer parlours were opened to the First Nations in the 1960s. This time, there were no North West Mounted Police to drive the whiskey traders away. This time, there were Mounties to arrest drunken Indians and put them in jail. Leo was one of them.

Over the years, he accumulated a record of alcohol-related offences. He was frequently jailed overnight for being drunk in a public place and released the following morning. But even then his cheerful personality and sense of humour eased the situation. Police officers who arrested him remember him as "an okay guy. He was never any problem. He wouldn't hurt a fly. There were never any charges of violence or anything like that." Sometimes older street people, like Leo, are picked up by police for their own protection against the weather or against those who would prey on them.

Sometimes Leo drank Lysol or Listerine, a thought that makes many drinkers grimace. But to the street people, Lysol and Listerine drinkers are nowhere near the bottom of the pecking order. That spot is saved for drug users. Leo never joined their ranks. He trapped a little and sold the pelts for enough to buy a bottle of Listerine by preference, if liquor was not available, and he drank with his buddies. Sometimes they drank on the riverbank, sharing whatever they had. Sometimes they drank at someone's house on one of the reserves or in town. He is remembered as a gentle loner. He rarely swore or used rough language.

The quiet loner became the prankster at times. One night he showed up at a Doug Bird's house on the Ahtahkakoop Reserve, south of Debden. The two men talked and joked and enjoyed themselves over a bottle of rye for hours. But Bird had promised to get up early to plant a garden for his wife, so the two men decided to make an early night of it. Leo had volunteered to help and sure enough, bright and early, he was up and ready to work. He was an excellent gardener, he assured his friend. While Bird went to the store, Leo began with the potatoes and was very quick. In fact, when the friend returned an hour later, the entire carton of seed potatoes and vegetable seeds was planted and the gardening was done. How it was done became clear a few weeks later. Doug Bird was not amused to find all the plants were sprouting in one small place where Leo had dumped the entire carton of seed.

Leo thought it was a grand joke. He laughed, ducked, and ran whenever he saw Bird after that. Bird was angry for awhile, but he said no one could stay mad at Leo. "He was crazy, that Leo! But he was a gentle man. And then, do you know what he did the next day? He borrowed a truck and came back and took all my beer bottles to cash in. He was crazy that guy! People here still call him 'My Gardener.'"

But alcohol abuse is not a joke anywhere and especially not on a reserve where, combined with poverty and hopelessness, it leads people into the criminal justice system. While First Nations people make up thirty percent of the population of Prince Albert, they account for eighty-five percent of the jail populations on average. Nearly half of the inmates in federal penitentiaries in Saskatchewan are Indians. Nearly one hundred percent of their crimes are committed while they are under the influence of alcohol, drugs, or both. Before the First Nations people were allowed to drink, they formed only a tiny percentage of jail populations. Jail was dreaded above all else in those times. The kind of incidents that led to jail sometimes led to greater tragedies. People on the Sturgeon Lake Reserve, fifty kilometres west of Prince Albert, remember a man who could not watch his sick cow suffer any longer, so he killed it. But slaughtering cattle without permission from the Department of Indian Affairs was a criminal offence. He was reported and charged but he could not face jail so he took his own life.

The government does very well from alcohol — it brings in taxes, and it provides employment for those hired to administer justice. Alcohol is seen by some First Nations people as another means of controlling their people. One elder describes it thus: "Your people built schools and they could not hold us. They built hospitals and they could not hold us. Now they build jails to hold us."

As in all nations with alcohol abuse problems, it is the children who suffer most. On the Big River Reserve, the children of *Se Se Wah Hum* school have written a creative play/dance they put on for parents and at cultural events. In their performance, a young girl and her friend, in traditional dress, approach other groups of actors who represent their drinking, gambling, glue sniffing, and drug abusing relatives, and beg them to come to a powwow and dance instead. "Return to the old ways," the children urge in their dance. Unfortunately, the children know firsthand about the realities of their performance. Leo never saw the dance performed. It began a year after his death. But he had a deep fondness and a deep concern for the well-being of children. Perhaps the dance might have returned him to the Sweet Grass Trail. Perhaps not.

There are many different paths an Indian can take during the journey through life. The ideal is along the Sweet Grass Trail to a successful old age in which one need not fear anything in this life or in the life to come. The choices are clear: the paths to choose from include alcohol or drug abuse, cancer, AIDS, or suicide. Or they can be paths of study, work, marriage, and healthful living.

The Medicine Circle is the guide to the proper way to live. There are prescribed stages in the circle that people must balance successfully to close their own life circle and successfully reach the end of their own Sweet Grass Trail. The circle has four stages: the buffalo, which represents learning and acquiring skills; the eagle, which represents farsightedness and planning; the mouse, which represents acquisition of material goods, including a home of one's own; and the bear, which represents parenting.

Leo did not reach the goal of eighty years and a completed circle. He had some skills and education, a home and sufficient goods for his pleasure, and a child. But he did not have a wife, and his child was not with him in his home. That Leo had walked the road of alcohol abuse is undeniable. However, if he had lived, he might well have returned to the Sweet Grass Trail. He might still have completed his circle properly and brought balance to his life.

Indian religious belief holds that how one conducts one's life will affect what ultimately happens. Taking care of health and physical well-being is important. Making positive changes in character and behaviour is too. However, it does not follow that all misfortune results from one's own actions or choices. It was not Leo's alcoholism that caused his death, although the two witnesses, Gar Brownbridge and Russ Yungwirth, say he was drunk when he entered the gun shop. Evil can enter into a person's life and end it. Sometimes this is because of some wrong action by the victim; sometimes it is purely the fault of the evil the victim encounters.

CHAPTER EIGHT

The Cree

Leo LaChance was an Indian man and that is not at all like being a white man. He could not measure himself by a white yardstick and he cannot be measured, living or dead, by white standards. Carney Nerland shot a stereotype dead. He had no conception of the man he shot.

In 1626, Father Le Caron told zealous young missionary priests in the New World that if they wished to become martyrs to their faith, they would be disappointed; the Indians allowed everyone to have his or her own faith. Leo LaChance would probably not have argued that Nerland's beliefs were wrong. The white man could believe whatever he wished. LaChance had his own values and those values were based on the experience of his own people and their thousands of years of life and death on this continent.

Nerland's creed is based on the theory of supposed superiority of whites over other races. Indian faith is based on the equality of all living things, including humans, which forms a circle, a chain. When one link is broken, the chain, the circle, is broken. All life has value.

Leo LaChance was born a Roman Catholic and was buried in the tradition of that faith. But he was also a believer in Indian ways and Indian faith, which shows great respect for the dead, for a belief in immortality, and for a God. One God. Traditional Native people hold all life and the Great Spirit in reverence. Things are done with prayer and respect.

The experiences in seventeenth century Paris or London were unsuitable and frequently useless in the New World. Without the patience and guidance of the indigenous peoples, the whites could not have survived in the wild, unfamiliar land. The Native people helped the newcomers at every step, even though they privately thought the newcomers were rather weak and silly. For their part, the whites told the Natives they were pagans and savages in need of civilizing.

The Native people settled the land and developed trade and political agreements that spanned the continent. They had languages, religion, music, art, and cultures older than their conquerors, yet were believed to be inferior by Europeans. Over time Native cultures were quashed or ignored by those who came to teach them the words of Christ.

His neighbours say LaChance was reliable. He liked people and when there was trouble, he was there to do what he could. But there was more to him than an example of Christian ethic. He was a link in the chain of Indian people, Indian belief, and Indian life.

Three thousand years ago, it was the Navajo nation that occupied what is now Saskatchewan. The Navajo, one of the largest of the First Nations, now live in the American southwest on a reservation that centres on the four corners where Utah, Colorado, New Mexico, and Arizona meet. They are called the *Dineh* in their own language, a language related to the Dene or Chipewyan language of the people who now occupy the northern half of Saskatchewan. The Navajo gradually moved south, and over the centuries other First Nations moved onto the Canadian Plains.

Cree or Nehiyawok artifacts have been found at sites including La Ronge, which indicate that they occupied this province at least as far back as A.D. 900. The white man's history traces the Cree back to New York State thousands of years ago, but loses the trail there and cannot account for their origins. The Cree believe their people may have come from Mexico originally, migrated north and then east, following the mammals that were returning to North America as the Ice Age ended and the glaciers retreated.

Gradually, over the centuries, the Cree people travelled northwest from New York State. There are Cree nations settled all the way from Labrador to the Rocky Mountains. Currently, the Swampy Cree live in northern Manitoba. The Woods or Bush Cree bands are spread across the northern parts of Saskatchewan and Alberta, and the Plains Cree occupy the southern areas of the three prairie provinces. The Plains Cree dialect predominates in Saskatchewan south of Prince Albert National Park and the Woods Cree dialect north of the park's southern boundary.

During the early years of what is now western Canada, the Cree lived together in small bands of several, often related, families. One man was chosen as the leader, called the *okimaw,* based on his experience and skills. The bands tended to spend the fall and winter in the forest where the thick bush offered some protection against the winter storms and where game was more plentiful. The men trapped fur-bearing animals and hunted for bigger game to feed the family. The women went into the bush to bring back the animals the men had killed. In spring and summer small bands joined to form large groups and moved farther south to meet other Indian nations for religious and social events and for trade.

No part of the animal was wasted. Even the hooves yielded grease. Women cut meat into thin strips and dried or smoked it. They scraped, cleaned, and tanned hides to make clothes, tipis, or utensils. A pit was dug, lined with a hide, filled with water, and heated with hot stones from the fire and meat was boiled in the hot water. Women and children gathered firewood, moss, and berries in season and snared small animals for food. Rigorous, relentless hard work was required just to survive. It was a way of life carried out by all Indians until the 1950s and is still lived by some.

The Company of Adventurers of England, or the Hudson's Bay Company fur traders, as they came to be known, arrived on the shores of Hudson Bay in 1670, where they first met the Cree. Europeans found the Cree to be a healthy, vigorous, and friendly people but with firm beliefs as to how they would live their lives. The Cree immediately engaged in a lively trade with the Hudsons's Bay Company that continued until after the Second World War. Trade and communications with the fur traders moved the Cree from the Stone Age to the Iron Age, virtually overnight.

The Cree leaders were experts at trade and diplomacy, rivalling their counterparts in Europe in their acumen and vision. When the first Hudson's Bay posts were established and the need for furs made known, the Cree chiefs turned the European need into opportunities for First Nations people. They allied themselves with the Assiniboine and began moving inland along the major river ways, encouraging the Plains Nations to trade their furs in exchange for guns, iron kettles, hatchets, axes, knives, and traps purchased from the HBC forts. The Cree traded fourteen beaver pelts for a gun and traded the gun to the Blackfoot, Stoney, Flathead, Kootenay, Shoshone or Peigans for fifty beaver pelts. In this way they controlled the distribution of guns to other tribes, which made them formidable players in the politics of the west. At the same time, the Cree traded along the Missouri River with the more sedentary farming nations, of the Mandan and Hidatsi, for corn, beans, and furs taken in trade from still other Indian nations. The Cree were soon established throughout the Plains as traders to be reckoned with and were considered better allies than enemies. Cree alliances played a role in the fortunes of their frequent enemies, the Blackfoot of Alberta. If the Cree sided with the Crow of Montana, the Blackfoot were in trouble. If the Cree attacked the Gros Ventres, the Blackfoot retaliated against the Cree.

The middleman system worked well, but it needed to be changed when competition with the North West Company forced the Bay traders to build forts inland along the Saskatchewan, Assiniboine, Churchill, and Nelson rivers. Now the Plains tribes, all the way to the Rocky Mountains, could trade directly with the company. Guns, previously available only to the Cree, were suddenly accessible to all. During the eighteenth century the Blackfoot and the southern prairie nations also had a temporary advantage over the Cree by being the first to own horses.

Once again, the Cree adapted their way of life to meet the challenges of changing economic conditions. Gradually, more bands remained on the prairies throughout the year instead of moving back into the forests in winter. While the Woods Cree remained fur trappers and traders, the Plains Cree became professional buffalo hunters. The split was complete by 1850.

When the Plains Cree moved away from the Woods Cree in the midnineteenth century, the two groups came to speak of each other as the Downstream People and the Upstream People. The Upstream People occupied the northern and western parts of the province, including the Prince Albert area, and the Downstream People occupied the southern and eastern portions.

Over the centuries, the fur trade became the parent of a new nation. Both English and French traders intermarried with the First Nations and the result was a new people, the Métis. They also became fur traders, trappers, and buffalo hunters. Some began to farm along the banks of the rivers throughout the prairies.

Numerous wars marked the period that saw the Indian nations struggling to control first the fur trade, then the horse trade, and finally, the buffalo. The last wars, the Buffalo Wars, were waged in the midnineteenth century. The battles were desperate, savage, and, in the end, unwinnable. A Cree band, camped at Fort Carlton, sixty-four kilometres southwest of Prince Albert, was attacked by a war party of Blackfoot, Shoshone, and Gros Ventre in 1848, but the battlegrounds were constantly moving south and west of Prince Albert. The buffalo had disappeared from the area by 1850 and local bands followed them into Alberta.

The final, major battle between the Cree and the Blackfoot was fought at Fort Whoop Up on the Old Man River in southern Alberta in 1870. The Blackfoot and their allies had more modern rifles obtained from the American traders, while the Cree still used aging flintlocks and muzzle loaders obtained from the Bay traders. The river ran red with the blood of more than two hundred dead and dying Cree. Three of the best known Cree chiefs were among the warriors fighting fearlessly that day: Big Bear, Piapot, and Little Pine. These three chiefs would lead their people through the difficult years ahead as the buffalo disappeared and the treaty negotiations began. In the end, after the last battle, the Blackfoot allowed the Cree to follow the last of the buffalo across Blackfoot territory and into Montana.

For centuries, the Prince Albert area has been a meeting place for First Nations social gatherings. Major powwows and the Indigenous Games draw together First Nations people from all over North America. During the fur trade years, it was a stop-over on the commercial routes of the Cree. The point of land that slopes upward at the forks, where the North and South Saskatchewan rivers join to form the broad Saskatchewan River fifty kilometres downstream from Prince Albert, offers a natural fortification. The width and speed of the river, at the juncture where prairie and forest meet, was never a barrier to the Cree. It was a part of their past, featured in the stories they told their children. Its Cree name is *Kisiskatchiwan,* which means fast flowing stream, and it was a part of the history of the LaChance family and of the Big River/Whitefish Cree Nation. It became a strategic camping place during the frequent wars that marked the end of the old, free way of life.

A more deadly foe emerged early in the relationships with the Europeans. By 1781, smallpox had killed more than half the Cree. Over the next one hundred years, smallpox, scarlet fever, diphtheria, and tuberculosis followed the trade routes across the west, slashing the population of the First Nations drastically.

The second wave of white people the Cree encountered were the missionaries. They did not view the Indians the way the fur traders did: as neighbours and business partners. The missionaries saw the Cree and the other Plains Nations as dirty, lazy, pagan children in need of a good dose of Christian ethics. Although motivated by Christ's commandment to love their brothers as themselves, they never quite managed to see the First Nations as brothers, but rather as sons and daughters. Red people were not considered equals by white missionaries.

On the other hand, the red people did not consider the whites to be their equals either, but, by the late 1800s, the foreigners had the upper hand. The buffalo were gone, the people were starving, the settlers were coming, and the missionaries were believed to have the knowledge necessary for the Cree's next major adaptation. Missionary annual reports cheered people back east as the number of converts increased regularly. They became Christian, they did not stop being Cree.

Autumn 1732

The band was in luck when it reached the shore of the North Saskatchewan River. It was warm and sunny for a morning in the last quarter of the Hunter's Moon. The river was low and it would not be as difficult to cross as it would have been in the spring when the waters could run high and very fast.

A young hunter and his family were travelling south with five other families, forty people in all, members of a band that hunted and trapped together all winter. The runners had arrived weeks earlier with gifts of tobacco to announce the medicine dance that would be held just across the river, on the flats at the base of South Hill. Already, other families could be seen moving among the tipis across the river. The young hunter went with his father and his younger brother down to the edge of the river to cut willow wands. Meanwhile, his mother, sister, and grandmother slid the heavy packs from their backs and removed more baggage from the dogs and their travois. The women unrolled a rawhide on the ground, laid out several long strips of leather and sorted the bundles in preparation for the trip across the river.

The father and sons climbed from the muddy riverbank with willow wands to make the *pitikonakana*, a small, round boat to ferry their goods across the river. The older boy squatted on the ground and held a big wand in a circle while his father fastened it together. The boys helped hold more willow wands in place while their father pushed and pulled and fastened them to the circular rim to make a large, round, deep basket, covered with the rawhide the women had prepared. The two long strips of leather were tied securely to the little round vessel and shorter strips were tied around the edge for the women and children. Like a large shopping basket, the bent willow container was loaded with the bundles the family carried. In the past, all of the children had ridden across rivers many times in other *pitikonakana* to other tribal gatherings. This time, they were old enough to swim with the shorter leather strips held in their teeth. The father fitted the two long leather straps across his shoulders and chest and prepared to enter the river. He sluiced the chilly water over his arms and some into each nostril before striking out for the far shore. His family joined him, the women and children swimming alongside the little boat, holding the thongs to help pull the little vessel and to keep them from being carried away by the strong current.

The young men of the band were always the last to swim across, herding the dogs ahead of them. As usual, N'Keem ran stiff legged along the bank, rushing to the water and backing away with her tail and ears back as the young hunter called to her from the shallows. "What kind of dog won't swim, you silly old girl?" He picked her up and carried her, squirming, into deeper water and then pushed her off, paddling downstream of her so she would not be swept away and could not head back to the shore.

Every autumn, the medicine dance provided an opportunity to meet with distant neighbours. The Cree bands from the south came to trade antelope and buffalo meat, fat and marrow and buffalo hides for venison, deerskins, herbs, berries, and fish. The natural products of the grasslands and forests were the subjects of brisk exchange as the two peoples prepared for winter. High on the women's list of supplies for the long cold months were the medicines that could be obtained from the medicine men during these autumn gatherings.

As the women and children erected the tipi within a circle, with the doorway facing east to greet the dawn, the young hunter helped build the medicine lodge, a long tent with a pole running from end to end about one metre off the ground. On the pole, the medicines were hung for barter and the medicine men sat below their wares on whole bearskin rugs spread on the ground. The art of healing using natural substances was well known to everyone. Knitbone or comfrey leaves to heal wounds and broken bones; Labrador tea for stomach, skin, or nerve problems; burned mullein leaves for lung and bronchial congestion or applied for pain or to stop a discharge.

The medicine men had devoted a lifetime to studying nature and developing complex medications and drugs capable of curing more serious diseases and injuries. They were natural scientists, not magicians or sorcerers and their science was deeply tied to the spiritual beliefs of the people: medical and spiritual advisors together in one man. If a man chose to belong to a medicine society, he had to pay a fee of eight articles of value. If he were accepted, then he would have to endure tests and initiation that were exceedingly dangerous. The medicine men would test their medicines on him and then revive him during a dance held in the medicine tent. When initiations were being carried out, the men were allowed to watch but the women and children were kept away for their own safety.

In the past, the young hunter had watched the dance in fascination but he had no intention of allowing someone to inflict sickness on him just to be able to learn how to prepare prescriptions. He would buy his medicines readymade and concentrate on getting into the warrior society. Besides, he was young and healthy so what did he need that stuff for anyway? If he got hurt then he knew what to do, what herbs to pick, how to make a gift of tobacco to the earth for their healing powers and how to apply them to heal his wound.

Medicine dances were interesting to watch, but they were not as much fun as spending time with the men. Two other young men his age had guns. That was what he wanted: a gun. The story going around the camp was that his cousin Saukamappee had recently fought in a war against the Snake Indians near the Eagle Hills, west along the river

— several days' journey away. Saukamappee and nine other Cree had guns to aid their Peigan allies against the Snake. Within hours, the Snake were beaten and driven away. When Saukamappee arrived at the medicine dance, they would all hear the details. The whites had guns, but they cost fourteen beaver pelts. The young hunter would have to be very lucky and work very hard on his trapline this winter if he was to have any hope of getting a gun from the Hudsons's Bay Company trader.

In the meantime, he was here to dance and have fun — standing around watching people haggle over medicine was not his idea of fun. He left and went back to the edge of the camp where the others were gambling on knife tosses or wrestling with each other.

His mother and grandmother were anxious to acquire more buffalo fat than they had obtained the previous autumn. They walked about within the circle of tents, discerning what each woman from the south had to offer and who she was, so they could decide how to get the most for the dried venison and soft doeskins they had to trade. They noted with slight smiles that many women still cooked their stews in a hole in the ground, lined with a hide and heated with hot rocks, while they had a fine iron kettle from the Hudsons's Bay Company post. Mind you, if the right deal came along, they might even part with the kettle. There was lots of time to decide what trades they would make. Talking it over quietly, they returned to their tipi, glancing up now and then to watch the children. The youngest son was standing a little way off from where his older brother and his pals were laughing and talking. The daughter would be with her friend in a tipi, talking constantly and playing with their dolls. It was time to start the evening meal. The women wrapped the first medicines they had bought in small tanned hides and packed them away.

Later that night, the young hunter's mother and father talked about friends who had divorced, and the news upset his mother. The man had put his wife aside. The marriage was over and the woman had been sent back to her parents' lodge. The man would not be at the medicine camp either. He and his new wife were staying away. It was depressing news but soon stories of silly things that had happened over the summer had his mother giggling.

The days and nights were becoming much cooler, especially here by the river, away from the trees. Thankfully, the ghost dance was always held inside a large, covered, rectangular enclosure, with a fire at each end. All night long, the men danced quietly, one behind the other, around the circle. Two men were chosen to serve, and they continuously ladled out pemmican. The dancers, shrouded under blankets, handed the food to the people sitting at the edge of the circle. The dance lasted all night but ended before dawn; the ghost dance could only be held in the dark hours and was never held in the same spot again.

A day later, the young hunter stood with others near his father and listened with considerable interest. His father's friend was talking about going west to the Blackfoot camps in the spring to trade guns for pelts. A gun that cost them fourteen pelts at the trading post on the bay could be traded to the Blackfoot for fifty or sixty pelts, enough to buy four more guns. His father and the band *okimaw* seemed to be agreeing with the friend. The boy was excited. It looked as though they were going to paddle west to the Blackfoot camps. He would be required to paddle a heavy canoe filled with trade goods, but there were sure to be guns among the items and surely he could find a good reason to try one out, hunting for food perhaps. This was the best medicine meet ever!

That night it started to snow. It melted in the morning, but it was a signal that it was time to go back to their winter camp. The father only smiled and said nothing when he noticed the tiny puppy his small son had tucked into the *pitikonakana*. By afternoon, they were headed north through the forest and the men's minds were on their traplines.

In the spring, the young hunter and his father did travel to the camps of the Blackfoot. It meant weeks of paddling upstream along the North Saskatchewan, but it was only the first of many such strenuous trading expeditions. They did very well at this trade. The first year, father and son both had guns. Two years later, the young hunter even went to the fort at York Factory, on the shore of Hudson Bay. The Hunter's Moon of 1740 saw father and son on the shores of the Missouri River, sixteen hundred kilometres south and west of their winter camp, trading guns and furs for corn and cloth. Cree hunters and trappers were becoming well-known as savvy traders across the west and there is evidence they traded with tribes from as far away as Florida, meeting in the southeastern corner of what is now Manitoba.

Thirty-two years later, Cree traders returning from the south were near the forks of the North and South Saskatchewan rivers when they encountered the strangest creature they had ever seen. A Blackfoot was sitting on a great brown creature and laughing at their astonishment. He was happy to show them the animal's speed and agility and, incidentally, how well he rode the beast. It was a horse, and it would abruptly change Cree history. The young hunter's grandson made up his mind that he was going to have one of these wonderful creatures. He would have to work hard and be lucky in his trading to carry out his dream, but with a horse he could go so fast and go far. He would beat the other traders to all the best markets. He could chase after the buffalo and race the wind. He was going to get a horse.

Within two years, Cree hunters rode on horseback and were no longer trappers. They left the trapping of furbearing animals and the ever-diminishing beaver to their cousins in the north, while they moved farther and farther south and west onto the plains to hunt buffalo for food and for meat to sell to the Hudson's Bay Company men.

After that, their alliances with the Blackfoot, Stoney, Peigan, and Blood nations deteriorated as battles broke out over buffalo hunting and horse trading. Stealing horses became common. The Blackfoot no longer needed the River Cree. During the winter of 1815, the Plains Cree gathered together in a huge camp at the forks of the two Saskatchewan rivers to prepare for war with the Blackfoot. Although the proposed war of 1815 came to naught, the bitterness increased as both sides began to feel the pressure of the white man's world, the failure of the beaver supply, which all had thought to be inexhaustible, and the diminishing herds of buffalo. As the old economic order broke down, conflict grew among the various nations. The struggle between the Blackfoot and the Cree was particularly bloody.

The frustrations were only beginning; the worst was yet to come. In 1820, one third of the Blackfoot died in one measles epidemic. Some whites were suspected of spreading the disease by sending infected blankets to other camps. Throughout the eighteenth century, the Cree along the North Saskatchewan were moving from the forest to the Plains. While some bands returned to their winter camps, others remained on the open prairie. They adopted the style of tipi used by the Blackfoot. Rather than the "headless tipi" used in the bush to circulate the smoke before it was released, thereby combating the hordes of insects that plagued life in the bush, this type had movable flaps at the peak, to allow the smoke to be released as it rose. In a century, the Cree had absorbed stunning changes to their lifestyle and turned these phenomena — the gun, the horse, and the buffalo — to their advantage. They became an aggressive entrepreneurial nation, with ties across the continent. These changes sometimes cost them their alliances with the Blackfoot, the Mandan-Hidatsi, and the Sioux, but the Plains Cree emerged as strong a Plains Nation as any.

Men like the young hunter moved from snaring animals with leather thongs and saplings to using metal traps to hunting with guns. They had learned to hunt buffalo on foot, then to employ corrals, pounds, and cliffs to trap the animals for slaughter, and finally, to hunt the great beasts on horseback.

Their sisters married young men from neighbouring bands and like their mothers and grandmothers before them, and their daughters and granddaughters after them, led a life very different from white women's. Indian women had power and position within the band. Like white women, they worked long and hard but they had an equality with men, while white women were still chattels of their husbands, with no say in family affairs, much less in politics. Everyone in the band was valued, but the power of a woman was recognized by Indians. An elder described it as such: when a woman is away from the home, the man can cope and do all the necessary chores and care for the children. But when the woman returns, the home is lit up again and warmed by her presence. Peace and a sense of well-being return with her. Women's powers were also pragmatic. Their opinions were considered in decisions facing the band, and in the home. A grandmother's word was law.

The nineteenth century was a time of continual wars and shifting alliances as the spectacular days of the prairie Indians came to an end. The powerful Blackfoot and Cree nations were devastated by wars and crushed by diseases.

The LaChance family's ancestors were part of the Big River/Whitefish band, a Woods Cree nation, which centred on Whitefish Lake. The band hunted and trapped from Stoney (Delaronde) Lake north into what is now the Prince Albert National Park, and traded to the south at Fort Carlton. It is not known when they came to that area, but how the band chose it is still related by Cree storytellers.

A man named Ne May Kah lived at Stanley Mission. He was a Stoney Cree. He moved north from Stanley Mission to the south shore of Lake Athabaska, to the part called "the boggy place where the birch are." It is so boggy that you need snowshoes to walk on it they say.

Ne May Kah married there and raised several children. When he was getting old, he dreamed he would travel south. In his dream, he saw a lake where his grandchildren would grow up and prosper. So Ne May Kah started the long journey south with his family. When he arrived at Ile à la Crosse, he thought it might be the country he was looking for, but he had another dream in which he was told to keep going south. He came to Green Lake, but his dreams again told him to continue. One day, he came to the top of a big high hill and there, in front of him was his dream — Whitefish Lake.

Ne May Kah, called Netmaker, is buried on that hill overlook-

ing Whitefish Lake on what became the Whitefish or Big River Reserve
and it is there that Ne May Kah's grandchildren, great-grandchildren,
and great-great-grandchildren have grown up and raised their families.

Ne May Kah was an ancestor of Kinematayo, the chief who signed
Treaty Six for the band at Fort Carlton in 1878. Although many of the
Plains Cree bands who lived south of the fifty-third parallel signed in
1876, others followed the example of Crowfoot, the great Blackfoot chief
from the Alberta foothills, who insisted that the treaties not be signed
until the government assured no liquor would be given or sold to the
people. The Cree of Whitefish waited two years before agreeing to sign.
Treaty Six forbids the selling of alcohol on the reserves.

Although the reserve includes Whitefish Lake, many families remained forty kilometres northeast of the reserve at Stoney Lake, his-
torically the band's trapping area. The area was expected to be included
in the band's reserve, but for some reason it was never surveyed for that
purpose. While the families are members of the Big River reserve, the
land they live on is not officially part of it. The members of Kinematayo's
band, the Delaronde or Stoney Lake people that the LaChance family
belonged to, the Pelican Lake band, and the Big River band joined to
form the present-day Big River Cree Nation, and settled on the Big River
Reserve.

The band maintained its traditional means of support, hunting,
fishing, and trapping, and many still follow the band's ancient way of
life. It is getting more difficult, however, as the fish swim in polluted
lakes and the deer, elk, and moose have been thinned out by advancing
civilization. Some men have been taught by their fathers to hunt, fish,
and trap. Others have never learned. Yet it was these skills that kept the
families of the Whitefish alive during the decades of starvation after the
treaties.

Before the treaty, the Cree families from Kinematayo's band, the families of Kinematayo, Rediron, Netmaker, McAdam, and LaChance, got

their supplies for the winter's trapping at the fort in the fall. They needed tea, flour, tobacco, sugar, bacon, knives, an awl, cloth, and traps, sometimes purchased on credit to be paid for in the spring. Setting out together from the fort, the families separated as they reached their trapping territories and set up their winter camps. In the fall and early winter, the men and older boys hunted while the women and children gathered, prepared, and stored the food against the bitter winter. Sometimes, at Christmas, the families returned to the fort for feasts and celebrations. But just as often they stayed in the forest and went about their endless work.

In January and February, the brutally cold months, the animals are no more anxious to be about than humans. Those months were best spent indoors preparing traps and equipment, telling stories, and enjoying one's children. By March, when the animals were on the move again, the trapping began in earnest. The men walked their traplines on snowshoes, picking up the animals they had caught, skinning them, and packing up the pelts and edible meat. The traps were reset and the trapper moved on. Often he rolled up in a blanket and spent the night sleeping in the snow, waking in the morning to build a fire for a little tea and bannock before moving on again. Back in camp, his wife and children prepared and stretched the pelts. By spring, they could hope to have eight or ten bear, a dozen or more beaver, several lynx, marten, otter, fox, wolf, and several hundred muskrat furs to trade. In mid-November and again in mid-May, runners with dogsleds or canoes would appear to collect the furs and bring supplies. In June, the families were back at the fort to trade their furs and to enjoy the social season of feasts and dances at the fort or at Whitefish Lake camp. Occasionally, other bands sent runners bearing tobacco and the invitation to attend the ceremonies they were preparing.

Fort Carlton is a rather beautiful palisaded fort with four towers. It is near stands of trees that in summer appear to sail like huge ships through the waves of tall grass that extend for miles in every direction. This is the transition area between the treeless grass Plains of the south and the forests of northern Saskatchewan.

The fort is situated on a long gentle slope running down to the muddy banks of the North Saskatchewan. It is fifty kilometres from Prince Albert on the outskirts of Beardy's and Okemasis Cree reserves, which stretch east and south to the historic town of Duck Lake. Today one can visit the old Hudson's Bay trading post, preserved as an historic site by the provincial and federal governments. Hundreds of thousands of dollars' worth of furs are stored in the loft, just as though it were an April day of one hundred years ago when the river ice was breaking up and the furs were being readied for their journey eastward, where eventually they would adorn an English lady's cape or be made into a gentleman's felt hat.

Living nearer the fort were the bands led by Chief Ahtahkakoop and Chief Mistawasis. The followers of these two Cree chiefs also had friendly business relations with the Hudson's Bay Company at Fort Carlton, but theirs was a different arrangement. The two bands hunted buffalo for the fort and kept it supplied in meat, pemmican, and buffalo hides.

John Rowland was a factor at Fort Carlton in the 1870s. He and his family were born in the country, all spoke Cree, and considered the Indian families at the fort their friends. Thus it was that Rowland's young daughter Mary was able to successfully plead with both her friend Ahtahkakoop and her father to let her go buffalo hunting with the band one early summer.

The band moved south onto the open Plains. The ponies pulled travois, which were poles crossed and tied over their backs and dragged on the ground behind them. The tipi covers and belongings of the families were strapped onto the poles on slings made of hides attached to the poles. Men, women, and children walked alongside. Behind them, a screeching Red River cart carried the meat and hides home from the hunt.

After several days' journey, they reached a site west of present-day Saskatoon. The women established a campsite and the men went hunting until they spotted a herd of the great, shaggy beasts. They rode their ponies bareback in the midst of the stampeding herd and when they shot a fat calf or a young bull, they marked their kill by throwing a moccasin beside it. The women followed behind, searching out the family kills and beginning the lengthy job of butchering and skinning the animals, then cutting the meat into thin strips and drying it. It took days to complete the job.

The women made pemmican, the foodstuff that sustained the northern fur trade. First the meat was hung on racks to dry, and then laid on the grass. When it was completely dried out, it was pounded and flailed into powder. Throughout the drying process, the women had also rendered the fat and marrow that would be used to mix the powdered meat into pemmican. The women made sacks of the hides and packed them full, then sewed them shut and stamped the bags flat. If one of the sacks could be found today, its contents would probably still be edible.

After the hunt was over, young Mary Rowland and Ahtahkakoop's elderly sister walked out onto the prairie in search of water. The young girl preceded the old woman up the side of a coulee and stepped into the adventure of her life. There, facing her, was a wounded bull, pawing and roaring its fury. The girl moved as fast as she could, knowing full well neither she nor anyone else could outrun a buffalo. "Throw down your shawl!" the elderly woman screamed and the girl obeyed, throwing her bright red garment at the animal. The bull pawed and tossed. The few seconds' delay gave Diomme Laboucan, a Métis buffalo hunter, his opportunity — he rode to the rescue and shot the pursuing bull.

Mary walked back to get the water and picked up the remains of her torn shawl before returning to camp. When they returned to Fort Carlton, the tattered shawl flew as a flag during the feast and grass dance that Chief Ahtahkakoop hosted to celebrate the courage of young Miss Rowland and her gallant defender, Diomme Laboucan.

CHAPTER NINE

The Missionaries in Prince Albert

In 1866, Reverend James Nisbet, his wife, and party left the Red River Settlement near Winnipeg and made their way to Fort Carlton. They were met there by George Flett, a Hudson's Bay employee from the fort, and two farmers from the Prince Albert area, Adam Isbister and Oliph Olson, who helped them to locate their mission for the Indians Nisbet longed to serve. The meeting had been arranged by the Presbyterian mission society, which had granted Nisbet's wish to found a mission in the Northwest Territories.

The first potential site Nisbet was shown was Whitefish Lake, north of Fort Carlton, across the North Saskatchewan River, the same Whitefish Lake that later became the centre of the Big River Reserve, the home of the LaChance family. Although there were quite a few Cree families in the area, it would have been necessary to clear a road from the Green Lake Trail in to their settlement. As well, it was considered not as suitable as another location where the farm land was exceptionally good — the flats on the south side of the North Saskatchewan River, the future site of Prince Albert. If Nisbet had chosen differently, then the LaChance family would have been part of a Presbyterian flock rather than Roman Catholic. There were already several farmers established close to the chosen site and it was near enough to the Sturgeon Lake, Fort à la Corne, Mistawasis, and Ahtahkakoop Cree bands to be suitable for a mission.

The area had originally been settled in 1862 by James Isbister, an English-speaking halfbreed and, like his father, an employee of the Hudson's Bay Company. Like most children of employees, James had been educated and then hired on when he was old enough to begin work. He was an intelligent man who made a success of fur trading and farming; he served as an interpreter and gained a reputation in the northwest as a musician and storyteller. His farm was near the present site of the Saskatchewan Penitentiary. When Isbister moved on in 1866, it was taken over by several Red River Métis families.

On 26 July 1866, Nisbet came ashore at the bottom of what is now Central Avenue and soon began to build his home and a church near the river. He named his settlement Prince Albert in honour of Queen Victoria's consort and proceeded to make his dream of a farm-based mission and industrial school for Indian children come true.

The decision to settle where he did was influenced in part by the fact that none of the bands in the area were anxious to welcome missionaries, and because the treaties had not yet been signed, the Indians expected to be paid for mission land. The Prince Albert site was not on Indian land per se and, in Nisbet's view, was still a suitable place for Indian children even though it was not close to any band. Once Indian parents were persuaded to send their children away to be educated, one place was as good as another, he reasoned. There was a campsite frequented by many bands three kilometres west of the new mission, approximately where the penitentiary now stands. It was not a permanent camp and it was some time before several Indians, most of whom were crippled or ill, settled permanently near the mission.

Nisbet was quick to judge the Indians he met and to conclude that they were obnoxious and more interested in food than in religious instruction. They were going to be "a troublesome people," more difficult to bring to civility and Christianity than he had thought. His task was made more difficult because he did not speak Cree, nor was he interested in learning the language or the culture. While the Cree families travelled many hundreds of miles in the neverending task of finding and preserving food for the long western winter, Nisbet saw them as lazy and self-indulgent, always drifting off somewhere. He concluded that Indian children were "wild things" in need of the discipline of his school.

The Indians were not slow in sizing up Nisbet and his party either. At their first meeting, one headman predicted that the Presbyterian minister was the forerunner of an army of settlers who would grab Cree lands. Nisbet denied the accusation outright. The Indian merely smiled and left. Within a year, Nisbet was speaking and writing of his hopes for a thousand settlers to reap the benefits of the rich land he had settled and the town he had founded. By 1881, there were more than three thousand people living in Prince Albert.

But it was a mistake to think the Indians were a simple people. They were, and are, a highly complex society that most outsiders do not see or understand. And the chiefs of the bands on the Plains had no illusions; they knew that their way of life was coming to an end. For one thing, the buffalo had already gone from the Prince Albert area long before 1866. Six years before Nisbet's arrival, an American had invented a process that used buffalo hides to make leather goods. With a steady demand for boots, saddles, and equipment for soldiers during the American Civil War, the assault on the buffalo by white hunters intensified. As whites moved in, the Plains Indians of the western United States prepared themselves to fight this major threat to their way of life.

Everything depended on the buffalo, a fact not lost on the American government. When the Civil War ended, the American armies were sent to slaughter the buffalo to force the Indians into submission and onto reserves. The effect was soon felt on the Canadian Plains, because the vast herds had always migrated on a predictable route across the border. Bands from the Prince Albert area were forced to travel all the way to Montana to hunt buffalo that once had roamed the banks of the North Saskatchewan.

The need to learn to grow food from Mother Earth had been a subject of discussion among the First Nations for many years. The chiefs had pondered how they would lead their people into a new way of life when none of them had any experience of farming or an agricultural society. With or without Nisbet, the Cree were going to endure an overwhelming change.

For centuries, the Plains Indians had enjoyed freedom to pursue their lifestyle, unimpeded by white intervention. Their relations with the Hudson's Bay Company had taken the form of a business partnership and they had the respect and friendship of the men they traded with at the forts. Now they were encountering very different relationships with whites. Missionaries saw them as "heathen" and childlike. Settlers saw them as lazy, dirty nomads. Very early the seeds of racism and resentment were firmly planted in prairie soil.

Nisbet and many others who came to "civilize" the red man had no idea of the real needs of the Plains nations. Christianity was not an answer. The First Nations had a religion that permeated every part of their lives and sustained them. Schools were not an immediate requirement. Indian children had to know how to live a proper life and how to hunt, gather, and prepare food and clothing for themselves. They were taught by example and not by guilt and punishment that the "spare the rod and spoil the child" philosophy of the white man maintained.

There were some whites the Indians looked to for help. The First Nations had welcomed the North West Mounted Police because they wanted the whiskey traders controlled, and a few policemen, Superintendent L. N. F. Crozier was one, argued with the government on behalf of the Indians.

In the 1870s, missionaries approached Chief Ahtahkakoop, near Prince Albert, wanting to convert his band. Ahtahkakoop was willing, but he insisted that the missionaries stay and explain the new religion they preached. He turned away several before he welcomed Reverend John Hines, an Anglican missionary and his assistant, David Stranger, a Manitoba Swampy Cree, to stay with the people and provide religious and academic instruction. Many missionaries, such as Hines, John MacKay, and others, were welcomed as friends because they met the First Nations people as equals and had an appreciation of the society that welcomed them. Nisbet gained little of that respect and friendship because he never really bothered to know the people he had prayed to serve.

Several Cree families, who worked at the mission had made the trip from the Red River area of Manitoba with the minister and his family and settled near the mission. Many had farmed in Manitoba and took up the same occupation east of Prince Albert while at the same time working for Nisbet. They became part of the Muskoday Cree Nation and are still known for their farming ability.

One of these persons, Mary Bear, was a nurse at the mission and cared for the Nisbet family as well. In 1924, when a plaque was dedicated to all the founders of the city, Mary Bear spoke of the arduous journey and the history of the settlement in French, Cree, and English. Her family believes her name is not on the plaque with all the others because she was Indian and Roman Catholic.

The women of Prince Albert and the women of the Big River Indian band had one thing in common: every day was a busy day of providing food, clothing, and care for their families. While Prince Albert women made dresses, pants, and shirts of cloth purchased at the general store, Big River women sewed clothes from hides they had laboriously tanned themselves. Many Cree women still know how to tan hides, but few relish the backbreaking task of scraping, smoking, washing, soaking, wringing, and stretching the skins to the smooth suppleness necessary for sewing them into garments.

While the women of Prince Albert gardened, collected chicken eggs and milked cows, the women of the band gathered duck eggs, plants, and berries from the forest and meadows, according to the seasons. While the women of Prince Albert salted beef, the women of Whitefish Lake cut fish and meat into thin strips, smoked or dried it, and put it away for winter.

While Prince Albert residents responded happily to an evening of fiddle music and recitations, the members of the band enjoyed family gatherings, storytelling, and feasts featuring delicacies such as moose nose soup. The Cree combined their religion and their celebrations of joy at powwows, sun dances, tea dances, and other seasonal religious celebrations. While Prince Albert residents resorted to the medical supply box or a doctor, if one was available, the people of Big River band drew on the medicines available in the forest or fields or called upon the medicine man.

The medicine men had great powers to cure and heal, but they could not overcome the epidemics of white diseases. By 1870, when smallpox was again devastating the prairie nations, Nisbet inoculated 130 Cree against the killer disease. All the Indians in Prince Albert area survived the epidemic, which took a particularly high toll among other First Nations in the Northwest Territories. Some missionaries provided medical aid for diseases for which the First Nations people had no immunity. The aid was welcomed but not blindly accepted.

By 1870, the Hudson's Bay Company had sold its right to Rupert's Land to the Canadian government. Originally granted by the British monarch, this vast area was bounded by the waters flowing into Hudson Bay. It was occupied almost entirely by First Nations and it was incomprehensible to them that land the company did not own could be sold to the Government of Canada. For the Woods Cree, this meant the fur trade as they had known it for centuries and, more importantly, the freedom of the land they knew for centuries had ended. For the Plains nations, the buffalo hunt as a way of life was over. Now they were faced with emissaries of the Dominion of Canada who said the Great White Mother required treaties of her children.

It is difficult to comprehend the dilemmas facing the Cree people at treaty time. It was not a matter of whether local bands would sign the treaty. They no longer had a choice. With their means of livelihood gone, they were near starvation. They had foreseen the disaster at hand as early as 1859 and had considered how best to adapt their ways to the sedentary agricultural life.

The problems facing the Cree leaders were staggering. Since they had no concept of land ownership, signing away their land was incomprehensible to them. They knew virtually nothing of farming and had no idea what to ask for, yet they had to make immediate decisions regarding the well-being of their people and the generations to follow. There was no real way of knowing how much the government could be relied upon to keep its word, or if it would treat the Cree fairly. There were only the experiences of other nations — the Ojibway and the Saulteaux in the east — and that certainly was not encouraging. The best that could be hoped for was to get as much as those nations had received, and that was not much.

While the Cree were struggling with smallpox and the collapse of their economy, and six years after he established his mission, the Reverend Nisbet faced crises of his own in Prince Albert. His wife became unwell and he came under fire in a letter to the editor of a Winnipeg newspaper. A Mr. Bell criticized Nisbet for spending too much time farming and not enough time preaching. A lot of money had been spent and not one Indian had yet converted, Bell wrote. Bell's information was unreliable but his accusations received prompt attention from the mission committee of the Presbyterian church and, in the late summer of 1872, the Reverend William Moore was dispatched promptly to Prince Albert to investigate.

Because of his wife's deteriorating health, Nisbet had decided to return with his family to Winnipeg in August of that year. On the trail, however, he met Moore, and upon learning of the investigation, returned with him to Prince Albert, leaving his family to proceed east without him. Moore found thirty-two families in the settlement, mainly Indian and Métis. More than half of the children and eight boarders from distant reserves were attending the mission school. Moore approved of Nisbet's work, noting that more than five hundred Indians, at least some of whom had been converted to Christianity, visited the mission each year. Moore supported continuing the mission. He further recommended that a school where students could learn to read and write in their own language be established at the mission. Moore left behind Reverend Edward Vincent who would take over while Nisbet took his ailing wife from Winnipeg to Ontario to see her family. They returned to Prince Albert in 1873 but by the spring, Mary Nisbet was terminally ill. They returned to Winnipeg where she died 19 September 1874. Her husband followed her to the grave eleven days later.

Within three years of James Nisbet's death, his successors, the Reverend H. McKellar and John MacKay, were reporting to the Foreign Mission Committee that Prince Albert was no longer suitable as a mission to the Indians. The bands in the area had moved steadily westward in search of buffalo and gathered in the Prince Albert area only briefly each year, when, of course, the missionaries took every opportunity to preach to them.

By 1876, the town was a growing community of four hundred souls, many of whom had been baptised into the Presbyterian fold. In the year he served at the mission, Reverend McKellar baptised sixty-seven persons, twenty-nine of whom were Indians. Although the railways had not yet reached Prince Albert, many settlers had begun homesteading in the area, a prelude of what was to follow.

In 1876, the mission was proposing the separation of the Indian and Home (white settlement) missions because neither group understood the language of the other. George Flett, who had assisted Nisbet and spoke Cree, was now ordained and was successfully running a mission farther west at Fort Pelly. John MacKay, who had also been invaluable from the beginning because of his fluency in Cree and his "wide influence for good over the Indians," was also ordained and was soon moved to a neighbouring reserve. It was remarked in mission annual reports that a rival school had been opened by "another denomination." This was the Anglican Emmanuel College, just west of Prince Albert, established in part to produce Anglican priests from among the Cree people. The college later became the foundation of the University of Saskatchewan in Saskatoon, but at the time offered instruction and boarding facilities at Prince Albert. It is ironic that the schools were considered "rivals" in the Foreign Mission Field, in what is now the heart of Canada.

In mid-August 1876, Cree bands began to gather near Fort Carlton and to set up camps a kilometre from the fort gates. On 26 August, nine bands, comprised of less than one thousand people, signed Treaty Six. The territory that the Indians signed away forever spanned roughly one quarter of modern-day Saskatchewan and Alberta. In exchange, they received twelve dollars each, a land grant of one square mile (640 acres) per family (later reduced in some cases to 40 acres per family) on reserve sites of their choosing. If, however, the land was later needed for railways, settlers, mining, public works, or lumbering, it could be reclaimed by Her Majesty with the consent of the band. A promise was made to maintain schools on each reserve, to prohibit liquor sales on reserves, to provide the right to hunt and fish throughout the territory they were signing away, and to pay five dollars annually per person. By comparison, the Canadian Pacific Railway syndicate was given twenty-five million dollars and a land grant of twenty-five million acres in exchange for building a railway across the west.

In addition, the treaty said Her Majesty would provide fifteen hundred dollars' worth of ammunition and twine each year for distribution among the signees. Each family of five would receive four hoes, two spades, two axes, two hay forks, two scythes, a whetstone, and two reaping hooks; one plough and one harrow for every three families; a chest of carpenter tools, a crosscut saw, a hand saw, a pit saw, files, a grindstone, and an auger for each band; wheat, barley, oats, and potatoes for the acres broken; four oxen, one bull and six cows, and one boar and two sows per band. Each chief was to be given a flag, a medal, a horse, and a wagon. He would be paid twenty-five dollars per year and receive a suitable outfit of clothing every three years. A medicine chest for the band was to be kept at the Indian agent's office. In case of a calamity such as a famine or pestilence, the superintendent of Indian Affairs was to advise Her Majesty what help the Indians needed and she would supply it.

Once two or more reserves were started and cultivation under way, an additional assistance of one thousand dollars per year was to be paid for three years. The Indians agreed to obey the law and keep the peace amongst themselves, other tribes, and the remainder of Her Majesty's subjects.

Head chiefs Mistawasis and Ahtahkakoop, with chiefs Peeyahnkahnichkoosit, Keehoowahah, Ahyahtuskumikimam,

Chakastapaysin, John Smith, James Smith, and Chipewyan signed for the Carlton Indians 23 August 1876. On 3 September 1878 at Fort Carlton, Chief Kinematayo signed for the band later known as the Big River Cree Nation to which the LaChance family belongs.

The transition from hunters to farmers, however, was slow and the solution to the problem of hunger was not prompt. For several years, the bands continued to hunt while they were waiting for the surveyors to mark out the land for their reserves. The surveyors never did make it to Stoney Lake, although the Whitefish reserve was laid out in 1880. The farm equipment was even slower to arrive, and very soon the Indians declared that the treaty had been broken. The Canadian government determined that despite widespread starvation among the Indians, food would be given only if work was done. But, regrettably, because the equipment had not arrived, there was no work to do. Some bands managed to break farm land by hand and people survived by eating gophers and even their dogs.

The problem, like all political problems, had many sources. The government in Ottawa was primarily concerned with getting a national railway built, holding the Americans at bay while the west was opened up to homesteaders, and keeping the voters happy during tough times. The majority of Canadians had never seen an Indian and had only romantic ideas based on Buffalo Bill's Wild West Show and newspaper accounts of Indian massacres by American troops (and sometimes vice versa). That the Indians were literally starving was of little concern to the public or the politicians. And of course, Indians would not have the vote for another eighty years. Consequently, thousands starved to death.

One Indian man took matters into his capable hands and solved a problem quite simply, using the white man's ways to do it. He met an inspector of Indian Affairs on the road near Batoche, sixty kilometres southwest of Prince Albert. The Cree man promptly told the man he too was an inspector. He had been to visit his people and saw they were starving. The obvious solution was food and he demanded a requisition from the Indian Affairs official. He was refused, of course.

After all, he was only an Indian. However, he was also a fearsome and determined warrior "consulting with a fellow inspector" in a desolate place, which permitted him a certain irresistible charm. He got his requisition and a few days later, at Frog Lake, three hundred kilometres west of Prince Albert, he loaded a wagon with needed rations for his people.

Some Cree leaders, notably Big Bear, Poundmaker, Little Pine, Piapot, and Lucky Man, refused to sign treaties for some time. They hoped to forge a Cree territory that would give their people a stronger base from which to negotiate with the Canadian government. Thousands of Cree from across the province gathered in the Cypress Hills to hunt what buffalo remained and to discuss their dissatisfaction with the treaties. By that time, Edgar Dewdney was Indian commissioner. He was a powerful bureaucrat who controlled the distribution of food for a starving people. After the North West Mounted Police in the Cypress Hills were ordered to stop handing out supplies, the reluctant bands were forced to capitulate. Little Pine and Lucky Man signed in 1879, Big Bear and Poundmaker in 1882.

Big Bear did not give up hope of organizing a unified Cree nation with stronger bargaining power, and other band leaders were interested in Big Bear's proposals. In 1884, with his influence, Big Bear organized a sun dance to be held near Battleford, to be followed by the largest council of Cree leaders ever assembled. Dewdney was worried by this show of strength. He intensified his "submit-or-starve" policy and lobbied for an increased police force. As the sun dance neared, he tried to prevent some bands from attending by sending out the NWMP to order them back. One leader and his people, stopped by the Mounties at Duck Lake and ordered to return to their reserve, followed the order until they reached their home. There the band literally made a U-turn and went on to the sun dance as planned.

Big Bear's scheme was to revise the treaties by assembling the Cree in one large territory. The great chief's plan was foiled by one of his own followers, a hothead who struck an Indian agent who had refused to give him food. When the NWMP came to arrest the man, there was a near riot. Big Bear and some of the other chiefs managed to control the radicals; nevertheless, the old leader was discredited in the eyes of the Canadian government and his own people. The last attempt to organize the Cree nations peacefully and diplomatically came to naught.

What the white settlers thought of the terms of the treaty is not recorded. There seems to have been little immediate reaction. The Cree were still considered to be "obnoxious folk" and their absence from the town was not noted with any particular sympathy.

No sooner were the "obnoxious Cree" disposed of by being placed on reserves in 1878, than the dreaded Sioux, the very ones who had killed General George Custer, appeared on the horizon at Miller's Hill on the east side of the town. The following year, the Minnesota Sioux, who had established their camp next to the town, were joined by the Teton Sioux, bringing the total close to one thousand people. Coincidentally, Lieutenant Colonel W. Osborne Smith of the Canadian Army arrived the same month as the Teton Sioux. His mission was to arouse a little interest in the militia as a protective force and to get a company organized in Prince Albert. He was immediately able to raise two companies of cavalry and one of infantry. Two days later, arms and ammunition arrived at Fort Carlton for the fledgling force.

In those days the newspapers were notoriously biased when reporting events involving Indians. The battle by the American Seventh Cavalry at Little Big Horn was touted as a devastating massacre of the gallant General Custer and his brave American soldiers by the Sioux. The facts that Custer had made disastrous tactical mistakes and that roughly half his noble American troops were either Canadian or European were not mentioned. As a result, it was the lurid details of a massacre that fuelled imaginations in Prince Albert.

In 1878 the Sioux were not so much a real danger as a feared danger. They too were starving. They settled some distance from the town and immediately sought work on farms and in the lumber business. But their initiative and industry did nothing to change the perception that they were bloodthirsty warriors. It was thought they were heavily armed and ready to wreak havoc on innocent settlers. The Teton Sioux were accused of breaking into homes and stealing cattle, even though there was no proof.

At the end of October, a rumour circulated that a group of Teton Sioux had stolen some cattle, and tension came to a head. In order for the arms and ammunition at Fort Carlton to be distributed to the militia, government regulation required that three justices of the peace agree on the decision. However, there were only two justices of the peace in Prince Albert at that time, Charles Mair and Thomas MacKay, who also commanded the infantry unit. A town meeting was called and the two justices were sent to the territorial capital of Battleford to confer with Lieutenant Governor David Laird. Meanwhile, settlers went to Fort Carlton and got rifles without benefit of any justices of the peace and drove the Teton Sioux away.

Several days later, the North West Mounted Police arrived to find eighty-eight lodges of Sioux, not two hundred as rumoured, no injuries, no damage, no cattle stolen, and no one who seemed to know anything about the troubles supposedly brewing in Prince Albert.

A government soup kitchen, employment, and efforts by both the townspeople and the Sioux resulted in peace and relative comfort for everyone through the winter. In the spring, most of the Teton Sioux moved south, the police detachment closed, and the militiamen returned to farming and shopkeeping once again. The Dakota Sioux who remained were nearly all employed by townspeople and formed the base of the Wahpeton band now located north of the city. Nevertheless, the stage was already set for conflicting race relations between whites and Indians.

Settlers were improving their circumstances through their own hard work. The Indians were seldom seen at all and appeared indolent when they were. They did not want to be whites and refused the ample opportunities to "fall in with the tide that surrounded them" as the poet Charles Mair put it. These "shortcomings" gave birth to the belief that all Indians were parasites, living off the work and hard-earned taxes of the white settlers. The seeds of racism were becoming firmly rooted.

Race continued to be a preoccupation in Prince Albert after 1880, but now it was horse races along River Street that mattered. It was a burgeoning little town, constantly developing new industries, new farms and new schemes for grandeur. Charles Mair, man of letters, the man who helped foment the rebellion of 1869 in Manitoba by insulting everyone who lived in Red River, turned his literary gift in a new direction. He attracted a doctor and numerous other professionals and master tradesmen to Prince Albert. They were joined by Hayter Reed, the first lawyer, a former military officer and a powerful influence on the future of Indians in the territories as Indian commissioner following the rebellion. Mair was a poet and an astute and busy businessman with his two-hundred-acre farm and general store. He was a justice of the peace, wrote frequent letters to the editor, and was a leader in the social and cultural activities of Prince Albert.

In 1879, Miss Lucy Baker, a woman who would have great educational and cultural impact on the fledgling town, arrived in Prince Albert. When the family she was accompanying from Ontario decided to stay in Winnipeg, the intrepid Miss Baker continued her journey alone. Miss Baker had been educated in Canada, the United States, and France. She was fluently bilingual. She had taught in ladies' schools in New Jersey and New Orleans before escaping through Civil War blockades back to Canada. A teacher at the Presbyterian school, she soon lifted Prince Albert's cultural level to new heights with her interests in music and literature. Moreover, she was sincerely interested in the education of her Indian charges and did not limit her concerns to the town. She frequently visited the encampment to the west of the townsite.

In 1879, the bands of Cree had begun to settle on the newly established reserves near Prince Albert, and the Presbyterian church received quite a shock. The "obnoxious Cree," who were members of Chief Mistawasis's band, now asked Reverend John MacKay to establish a church on their reserve 113 kilometres west of town. To the astonishment of the missionaries, Nisbet and MacKay's teaching seemed to have a great effect on the band. Resisting all others — Anglican,

Roman Catholic and Wesleyan — they asked the Presbyterians to join them on their reserve.

But it was George Flett who gave the most insight about the Indian missions. In his report written in 1878, he pointed out that many were starving and cold. They had such inadequate clothing, he was forced to make two trips to outlying camps to bring about twenty freezing, hungry people to his own home where he cared for them for more than a month. As a result, the mission society was moved to send two hundred dollars to build a church at Flett's mission. The construction did employ a few of the Cree and lessened their hardships somewhat.

Meanwhile, MacKay concentrated on teaching Cree syllabics to the people of Mistawasis so they could read the Bible for themselves. Having at first neither a church nor a school, MacKay carried out his missionary work in his own parlour. His daughter Jessie taught thirty-nine pupils in their home without compensation from the mission board or the government.

In 1883, forty lodges of Dakota, or "heathens," as the missionaries put it, had been set up on Presbyterian property, bringing themselves to the attention of the mission but getting no further action than a note in the annual report saying that it "might be an idea to administer to them."

The needs of forty starving families was secondary to the more mundane concerns of central mission office and, apparently, to the Presbyterians in Prince Albert. What they were interested in was the sale of church lands to raise money for the building of a manse by the minister. He was relieved of his duties.

The next minister, Reverend W. McWilliam, was much disturbed by the "heathen Sioux" who were "still hanging around." The drums of the Sioux, as they engaged in their "idolatrous dances" disturbed Sunday services, but the "wails to the deaf gods" when one of the Sioux died particularly bothered McWilliam. He found it shocking they lived so near and yet no attempt was made to acquaint them with "the true religion."

It was Lucy Baker who came to the rescue. She had developed a deep interest in her Indian students and spent a great deal of time at their encampment west of the town. Soon she was visiting the Dakota camped on the north side of the river, although she was warned by friendly Cree to beware of the "vicious Sioux." She learned the Dakota language and paddled a canoe across the river regularly to teach those camped at what is now the "Little Red," a city park. She campaigned for the establishment of the Wahpeton Reserve for the Sioux and lived and taught there until 1905.

Jessie MacKay, daughter of the Reverend John MacKay at Mistawasis Reserve, had eventually acquired a school but because her pupils had only thin cotton clothing they were prevented from attending classes when the temperatures reached -45 and -60 degrees Celsius.

Between the lines of piety in the annual reports to the mission office, the worsening conditions for the First Nations was becoming apparent. MacKay, feeding many families at Mistawasis from his own pocket, asked for a raise and was denied. However, the board did decide to pay a teacher's salary to Jessie.

It was noted there was a crop failure on the reserve in 1884 but as the annual mission report stated: "Chief Mistawasis is a noble Christian man. He takes a sensible view of all questions affecting his tribe. He and his people are loyal to the government." Loyal but starving. Mistawasis realized the future of his people depended on learning what they could from the whites in order to survive in a white world. It earned him an interesting accolade: "Old Chief Mistawasis is a living refutation of the flippant jibe that the only good Indian is a dead Indian."

CHAPTER TEN

The Aftermath

For twenty years or more before the signing of the treaties in 1876, the Cree had been trying to limit the buffalo hunts because they could see the herds were diminishing rapidly. The buffalo were constantly moving westward, leaving Manitoba and then Saskatchewan virtually devoid of the great beasts. The Cree followed as the buffalo moved into present-day Alberta and Blackfoot territory in the 1850s and early 1860s.

As the situation worsened, the Cree banded together. In 1865, three thousand from Saskatchewan, including Ahtahkakoop's band from Prince Albert, trekked to the Cypress Hills in the southwestern corner of the province. This did nothing to improve relations with the Blackfoot, Peigan, and Blood Indians nor with the federal government. In fact, the concentration of Cree was a great concern to the government, even though it was obvious that starvation had motivated them. Indian Affairs Commissioner Edgar Dewdney did his best to disperse them by withholding food rations.

By 1879, the buffalo were gone from the Cypress Hills; only in Montana were there sporadic sightings. Forced to return to their old hunting areas, chiefs Big Bear, Piapot, and Little Pine decided to pursue the old idea of a consolidated Cree nation. Runners were sent out inviting all bands to travel to the Battlefords to discuss the scheme.

Driven out of the Cypress Hills area and defeated in the Battle of Belly River by the Blackfoot, the Cree had no option but to sign the treaties. But Big Bear, Piapot, Little Pine, and Poundmaker hoped a close alliance would at least give the Cree some bargaining power with the Canadian government. The lack of food was critical.

The Cree were not challenging a well-laid-out plan by the federal government. In fact, politicians and bureaucrats had very little idea about what to do with the aboriginals. Little forethought had gone into the needs and realities of aboriginal life. Despite hundreds of years of experience with First Nations in eastern Canada, and the reserve and residential school systems in effect since the 1600s, no other plans or research had been developed to deal with the Plains and Northern Woods First Nations of the west. One thing was certain though, Lieutenant Governor Dewdney and Commissioner of Indian Affairs Hayter Reed were not at all pleased by the spectre of a united Cree nation.

The First Nations were not the only people of the Northwest Territories to be unhappy with their current situation. White settlers in Saskatchewan were experiencing great difficulties with weather, land inspectors, and crops. There was a worldwide depression and the railways in 1880 had only reached Brandon, Manitoba. Dreams were running ahead of reality.

The Métis and other half-breeds had serious concerns of their own. Their communities had been established for decades before the white settlers began to arrive. Now the federal government planned to survey the new territories into square townships and it looked as though the Métis might have to fight for their right to keep their long, rectangular, river front farms, carved out of the wilderness years before without thought to surveys and homesteaders. The descendants of the fur traders and trappers and their Indian wives were in danger of losing their homes in their own homeland. They were not even counted as being there, even though James Isbister, an English-speaking half-breed, and his neighbours, the Fletts, Olsons, and MacKays, had settled in the Prince Albert area four years before Reverend James Nisbet "founded" the mission settlement. They were there when the settlement was established, yet only Nisbet is called the founding father.

In May 1884, Isbister was on his way to Montana with Gabriel Dumont and two other Métis. Their plan was to visit Louis Riel, the renowned Métis leader, and invite him to the Saskatchewan River area. After he arrived there, Riel did his best to convince the First Nations that it was in their interests to support the Métis cause. Riel told the chiefs that by taking over the territories and setting up their own government, they would get a better deal than they could hope for from the federal government. Chiefs Big Bear, Poundmaker, Little Pine, Ahtahkakoop, Mistawasis, and the leaders from the Big River and Dakota bands, from the Prince Albert to Battlefords area, did not agree with Riel. They believed their best hope lay in bringing about a peaceful agreement with the government and negotiating the best possible settlement of their grievances. The chiefs believed there was no possibility of winning a pitched battle with the government forces and no way to stem the tide of settlers soon to engulf them.

But while the majority of chiefs opposed Riel's ideas, members of each band argued in favour of an uprising. Riel at least offered some hope while the government in Ottawa did nothing to merit the loyalty of the First Nations people as conditions worsened in the west.

In Prince Albert, relationships between whites and Indians deteriorated further. The Cree were still considered an obnoxious people, difficult to deal with, and lazy. The Dakota Sioux, who had demonstrated quite clearly that they were a peaceable, hardworking people, were seen through the nightmare images of the Battle of the Little Big Horn. Although they had lived in the area for nearly fifteen years, the whites still did not realize that there were actually three bands of Dakota Sioux, not one. The whites refused to look realistically at the people who had worked for them for more than a decade, people who were successfully rebuilding their lives.

As the rebellion flared at Batoche and Duck Lake, just fifty kilometres away, the inhabitants of Prince Albert feared not the dreaded Sioux warriors, but their wives. It was rumoured that the Sioux women had bargained with their warriors to be able to come to Prince Albert to kill all the white women. Just how and why these mothers would leave their never ending tasks and their children to walk the many miles to town to cut off their source of income and ultimately their own lives, was not explained.

Although the First Nations had gotten on well with the Hudsons's Bay traders and factors for centuries and enjoyed mutual respect, the same could not be said of the government employees they were forced to deal with after the treaties, many of whom were enjoying political plums by being appointed Indian agents and farm instructors. While some were dedicated and fair, many were not. While some exercised common sense and compassion, others displayed an uncommon lack of sense and no compassion whatsoever. Even though the rules were made in Ottawa with no regard for the realities of life in the territories, some still applied them rigorously.

Ottawa's ignorance of their way of life led to disaster in 1885. The First Nations paid the price but the harvest of resentment has yet to be reaped. On a map of Saskatchewan, the areas involved in the rebellion of 1885 hang like two tear drops: one from Prince Albert and the other from the Battlefords.

Sarah Goodlad was seven when the rebellion broke out at Duck Lake. Her grandfather was a trader at Fort à la Corne and her mother, Mary, had been the first child born at the fort. With the other women and children in Prince Albert, Mary and Sarah found refuge in the Presbyterian Church, where a cordwood palisade had been erected. Sarah and her mother waited there, crowded and frightened. There were rumours and more rumours, built on the flimsiest of evidence. A lone Indian, spotted riding miles away from the town, was proof of an imminent attack by "the savages." The Dakota women were said to have won the right to scalp all the white women and children. The Blackfoot were riding to the aid of the Cree. Hundreds had been killed in other places. Finally, after a few days, when nothing had happened at all, the women were allowed to take their charges home again.

The residents of Battleford were having a much more frightening time of it. They were aware that Big Bear's warriors had killed eight white men at Frog Lake three hundred kilometres to the west. On 30

March 1885, the population of the town, with the exception of the lieutenant governor's cook, took refuge in the fort. All too soon, the Cree arrived in force at the fort gates. They were led by Big Bear, Poundmaker, and Little Pine, all well-known and respected in Battleford. The three leaders had chosen to go immediately to the Battleford government representatives and make it known that they wanted no part of Riel's rebellion, and that their loyalty was assured. Understandably, they also asked for food for their starving people. The government official refused even to leave the fort to talk to the Indians, much less give them the supplies they had required. Although the Hudson's Bay factor offered to provide beef, it was too late. The angry Cree ransacked the town but to their credit injured no one. In the centre of the melee, the lieutenant governor's cook calmly provided meals for any who asked.

Crowfoot had faced a similar set of circumstances but instead used the occasion to speak at great length about the loyalty of his people, deliberately refraining from mentioning their needs. The two situations ended very differently. Crowfoot was believed and his people rewarded (and bribed) with dramatically increased rations of beef and flour, through the foresight of a government official. The bureaucrat whom Big Bear, Poundmaker, and Little Pine were forced to deal with was anything but reasonable and farsighted.

The citizens of Prince Albert had reason to be frightened. Battles were fought all around them — to the south, at Batoche and Duck Lake, and west at the Battlefords, Cutknife Hill, and Frog Lake. But the residents of the seven reserves north and east of Prince Albert and three in the west all remained loyal to the Queen and faithful to the treaty terms.

Rebellion Epilogue

"Are you drunk?" asked the chief of the One Arrow Reserve near Batoche. He could not believe what the court interpreter had just told him. He thought the man must have been drinking to say such nonsense. Since One Arrow spoke no English a Cree interpreter was trying to explain to him the decision of the Regina court and the sentence. The elderly chief had been found guilty of treason/felony in English, a difficult concept to explain. There is no word for treason in Cree and so the interpreter explained to One Arrow that he had been found guilty of "knocking off the Queen's bonnet and stabbing her in the behind with a sword."

The court's decision was as bizarre as the translation to One Arrow, Big Bear, and Poundmaker, who were being punished for a rebellion they believed they had made every effort to avoid. The chiefs had seen that no good could come from war with the whites; that the repercussions would be swift; and that they had nothing to gain. There were far too many whites to hope their flood into Indian territories would end. But the chiefs had to deal with so many desperate situations. The great plans to make farmers of the Indians was far behind schedule because the instructors and equipment had not arrived. The government had said they planned to give the Indians food until they were self-sufficient, but someone somewhere had decided: no work, no food. The people were starving to death. The people of One Arrow Reserve were reduced to eating gophers. Many were dying. The young warriors naturally asked what had they to lose by rebelling?

The chiefs had taken the treaties seriously. They had smoked a sacred pipe, binding them to their promises on behalf of their people, forever. The government did not see it the same way, but the chiefs did not intend to break their oath. Surely the government could be made to see that their people needed help?

But the government refused to see. Big Bear made an impassioned plea for his people who had been scattered and were in hiding but it was ignored. He, One Arrow, and Poundmaker were imprisoned. Big Bear's band was never allowed to regroup and their reserve was taken away.

William Bleasdell Cameron told an interesting story of Big Bear in captivity. One day, his jailers found the old chief's locked cell empty.

Big Bear's son calmly told them his father was outside the prison. The guards rushed outside where they found Big Bear, sitting on a hill, looking out over the wide, free prairie. The guards had no idea how he had escaped to the outside from a locked cell in a penitentiary with high walls and locked gates. The guards, boxing him in on all four sides, led Big Bear back to the prison. Big Bear apologized and promised he would not leave without permission again. And yet, when the jailors reached the still-locked cell, they found Big Bear was already in it, chuckling about the Cree powers he possessed that could fool them so easily.

After three years in Stony Mountain Penitentiary, public protest led to the release of the three chiefs. One Arrow was ill and died in Winnipeg very shortly after. Big Bear returned to Saskatchewan and soon died. Poundmaker went to his home near Battleford and then walked to Crowfoot's camp near Red Deer, Alberta, to visit his beloved adopted father. He died there and was buried on a hill overlooking the Blackfoot camp.

The rebellion was an excuse to quell the First Nations once and for all. There would be no treaty revision and no autonomy for Indians. In fact, it was decided Indians were to be assimilated, and in the meantime they must stay where they belonged — on the reserves. One of the aftereffects of the failed rebellion was that the philosophy underpinning the reserve system changed. Instead of a jumping-off point where First Nations peoples could learn new ways of making their living as farmers, the reserves became virtual prisons. Since whites and First Nations seldom saw each other any longer, the negative attitudes engendered by the rebellion hardened and there was no real chance of reconciliation. The feelings of fear and anger have not lasted but the attitude of superiority has, and is part of today's racism.

At the beginning of the rebellion, there were nearly fifteen thousand First Nations people, forty-eight percent of the population in what is now Saskatchewan. They would not attain that number again until 1931, and by then they made up less than two percent of the people of Saskatchewan.

The First Nations were not only restricted to their reserves with their guns, horses, and freedom gone, but the government also began its policy of assimilating Indians. The children were taken away from their families and sent to boarding schools run by churches elsewhere in the province. There was no choice. Those who kept their children at home lost them anyway when the police were sent to take them away to school, and then the parents starved from lack of rations denied to them as punishment for breaking the law.

In white educational institutions, the children soon learned their parents were "pagans and heathens and all they believed in was wrong." An elder who has never before been at a loss for words was lost this once. "I cannot tell you what it is like to be told as a small child that your parents and grandparents, who mean everything to you, are both wrong and evil."

Not everyone found the residential schools so devastating. For many, it was an opportunity to eat regularly, wear warm clothing, and prepare for some kind of future. "I thought I had gone to heaven. We got three squares a day," is how one Native politician put it. For another, Jim Settee, whose father was the Anglican priest on Big River Reserve, the residential school at Onion Lake was a good experience. Settee was able to take part in the schoolwork, religious teaching, and agricultural training without losing his identity as Cree man.

But for many, it was a step into nothingness. They emerged neither Indian nor white. They had no experience of family, and became part of a generation that did not know how to raise children. They also had no idea how to be Cree anymore.

Life for the parents and others left behind on the reserve continued to be an endless struggle to survive, but now it was a struggle to survive in a world of agriculture of which they had no knowledge. No longer were they allowed to farm collectively. In fact, if they had purchased farm machinery together before the rebellion, then they were forbidden to use it. In an attempt to keep the Indians isolated and in disarray and to encourage them to follow the European peasant model, families were given small, individual plots of a few acres. They had one hoe, one shovel, one rake, and one flail to beat the grain from the stalks. There was an added cultural impairment. The men were traditionally hunters. Farming, for them, meant staying in a confined area and grubbing in the dirt at the behest of someone else. It did not come easily to them.

In an attempt to stifle their way of life, cultural activities and religious celebrations, such as the thirst dance, sun dance, or ghost dance, were forbidden. The government feared the ghost dance, which had been central to the disaster resulting in the massacre at Wounded Knee in the United States. Since it was believed to make warriors invincible and impervious to bullets it became a desperate last chance for liberation. The dance had surfaced in the prairies but after the rebellion it was quashed. The government was able to report, "Poundmaker and Little Pine's people in the Battleford area were now performing eight-handed reels and quadrilles and had really taken to the cotillion."

For Lieutenant-Governor Dewdney, the system seemed to be working well. The public was relieved that the savages were out of the way, even though the worst crimes they were accused of in the 1890s were the theft of a cake and a pan of gingerbread in the Battleford area.

In the eyes of the government, failed crops on an Indian reserve meant the Indians were not taking agriculture seriously enough. The NWMP pleaded with the governor of the North West Territories to reconsider their stand. The police argued there was no game, no food, and no crops so Indians were forced to steal cattle that ranged onto the reserves. Instead, rations for Indians were cut from a pound of flour and a pound of meat per day (if they were working) to a pound and a half of flour and a half pound of bacon (which Plains Cree hated) twice a week. In 1887, three thousand starved to death.

Although individual members of the NWMP still tried to help, relations between Indians and Mounties continued to change drastically. No longer were the scarlet-coated Mounties seen as benefactors sent by the Great White Mother to protect the First Nations from the evil others would do to them. Now they were the police who enforced separation of First Nations and whites, who kept the Indians on the reserves, who took runaway children back to school, and who upheld a law an Indian could never understand, the vagrancy law. Why should someone be put into jail for doing nothing?

On the Sturgeon Lake Reserve, some thirty kilometres north of Prince Albert, the Cree did not settle permanently until after the Rebellion. It was the lake, with its proximity to both forest and plains that caused the forefathers of the Sturgeon Lake band to choose the site of their reserve. No whitefish in the world tastes as fine as those taken from Sturgeon Lake Reserve, they claim. They wanted to be sure to provide for their grandchildren and their grandchildren's grandchildren.

Chief Ah-yah-tus-kum-im-am (baptised William Twatt) and his councillors placed their mark on the treaty on 3 August 1876. Some members had their doubts at the signing. Were interpreters Peter Erasmus, Peter Ballendine, and the Reverend John MacKay repeating everything they were told? Some of the promises they were repeating did not sound true. The band signed, despite their doubts, and remained in the area hunting and trapping in the north and fishing and hunting on the prairies. They were neither Woods nor Plains Cree, but adopted the best of both.

Like all of the other Cree bands, the Sturgeon Lake band felt the heavy hand of the government after the Northwest Rebellion. The regulations were restrictive and nonsensical. No one could leave the reserve without a permit, nor could they buy or sell farm products without a permit. Worst of all, they were not allowed to sell their cattle and soon the herd outstripped all the available forage. Still they were not allowed to sell any cattle. Anyone who slaughtered an animal, no matter what the need, was jailed. The band was reduced to trading cattle literally for a song. Some band members still remember trading animals with the Wahpeton Dakota (Sioux) band for some of that nation's traditional songs and dances. Finally, permission was granted to grow more hay at Sucker Lake nearby.

Of the local bands, perhaps the Muskoday band was the luckiest, although they too suffered from the government's intransigence. The band had an advantage over other Cree in the area. Many of them had been farmers in Manitoba before they migrated in 1866 to Prince Albert with the Reverend Nisbet. They knew what they needed. They formed a band at treaty time and eventually asked a Cree man from the Fort à la Corne band, who had been given the baptismal name John Smith, to be their chief. Smith's brother, James Smith, was the chief of the Fort à la Corne band. Searching for a suitable reserve, Chief John Smith climbed a ridge on the west side of the South Saskatchewan River, east of Prince Albert, and knew instantly he had found what he was looking for — Mus Kow Tay — flat grassland. The government called it Muskoday.

Those on Muskoday Reserve have always farmed successfully, sometimes despite government direction. In the early days, Muskoday farmers communally bought a threshing machine, a ten horsepower giant with two flywheels. In the 1930s however, there were tough times on the reserve, sometimes made worse by Department of Indian Affairs' decisions. At one point, there was only hay enough for half the cattle on the reserve. A request was put forward to sell part of the herd. Permission was denied and the Indian farmers were ordered to purchase feed for the animals. However, the hay they were able to buy was too coarse, cut too late. Many cattle died and the remainder were too thin by spring to bring good prices.

After the Depression, the lot of the Muskoday band did improve. In 1961, the band successfully negotiated a thirty thousand dollar loan from the government. If twenty thousand dollars were paid back in five years, the remaining ten thousand dollars would be a grant. The farmers paid it off in four years. There were ups and downs in the reserve's agricultural history, but in 1977, representatives went to Ottawa and successfully negotiated self-determination for the band. They opened their own bank, they had long operated their own ferry across the South Saskatchewan River, and, in 1965, they managed to switch from church-operated schools to those run by the band under the provincial education system. The result is a matter of pride — large high school classes and graduating students.

CHAPTER ELEVEN

The Gun Shop Owner

For awhile, in the late 1970s and early 1980s, the Crescent Heights area of Prince Albert wore a wide selection of swastikas painted on mailboxes, sidewalks, walls, and telephone poles. The neighbourhood was then a newly established sprawl of crescents and boulevards with neatly maintained middle-class homes and brand-new schools and playing fields. The neighbours were tolerant, and those on Cowan Drive and MacKay Crescent simply assumed it was that peculiar Carney Nerland behind the graffiti and chose to ignore it for the most part or discreetly wash it away. One night, racist slogans were pasted on the windows and outside walls of a small pool hall and video parlour an immigrant Vietnamese family had opened in the tiny mall on Twelfth Avenue East. Those who paid any attention assumed Carney Nerland was behind that too — he lived nearby.

Carney's interest in things Nazi had been evident from an early age in his army fatigues, jackboots, and his choice of reading material. At junior high school, he wore a uniform of his own devising, based on a Second World War German military style and he enjoyed disrupting class with racist jokes. Any teacher who paid attention to Carney's interests was soon shown reams of material on German military history, Nazism, or Carney's personal hero, Adolf Hitler. His teachers do not remember him being a happy, normal child after age eleven, at least not the way other boys were happy. Carney was bright and he did good work when the subject interested him. Otherwise, he was content to just cruise or ignore his studies. He paid attention to anything to do with war or violence, but then, many boys that age do.

Carney's mother is a Jehovah's Witness, so the boy had a strict religious upbringing. At school, he avoided all contact with Halloween, Christmas, birthdays, or singing the national anthem. Carney used religion when it suited him to do so. His father, Bob, did not seem religious — instead he had a big bad biker image. As a boy, Carney seemed to be very attached to his father, who was tough, aggressive and, in Carney's eyes, did important things. While Bob lived in Prince Albert, he drove trucks and wrote a column on motorcycles for the Prince Albert *Daily Herald* called "Fat Bob on Bikes." He did not get into trouble with the police but many of them knew who he was, and those who had any reason to stop him found him uncooperative. He was known for the German army helmet he wore in place of a motorcycle helmet. He was thought to be at least an associate member of an Alberta motorcycle gang. He did not like Indians at all.

Carney was not a discipline problem in school, but he was evasive and manipulative when confronted. He had an excellent vocabulary and used it to get himself out of trouble. Failing that, his mother could be counted on to visit the school in defense of Carney. He was not as attractive as his brother, Alfen, or his sister, Hali. For one thing, he was overweight. No one remembers Carney having any friends in school. He was seen as a loner and as a bully who picked on kids who were different. There were stories of children being pushed down the stairs at Riverside School and Jewish students being threatened and taunted by him.

By the time he was a high school student, Carney had learned to tone down his dress and his behaviour. He was quieter and less obtrusive, confining his zeal for Nazism to reading and collecting memorabilia and magazines. He became increasingly focused on right-wing philosophy and his mind was closed to any arguments against it. Partway through grade eleven, he quit school and got a job. He was like many Canadian students in the 1980s except for two things: his preoccupation with Nazism and the terrible hatred people saw in his eyes.

In the 1980s, Bob Nerland moved to Vancouver where it is believed he began an import business. Carney Nerland says he was initiated into the Ku Klux Klan by a Corrections Canada employee while he was in British Columbia with his father. Nerland said later he did not take the membership seriously. He thought it was a joke.

But if Carney Nerland can claim to have fallen accidentally into membership in the Ku Klux Klan, the same cannot be said of his entry into the Aryan Nations. In mid-July 1984, Nerland had attended, apparently of his own volition, a gathering at the Hayden Lake, Idaho, compound of the Church of Jesus Christ Christian Aryan Nations. The head of this deeply racist, white supremacist organization was Pastor Richard Girnt Butler, then in his seventy-sixth year. It was Butler who oversaw the construction of the church compound, with security as elaborate as a prison camp.

Richard Butler was once an aeronautical engineer whose interest in politics began with his admiration for Senator Joseph McCarthy and his zeal in hunting out Communists. Eventually Butler's philosophy moved so far right that he became enamoured of the California-based Church of Jesus Christ Christian. The sect believes that the British and selected colonists are the true descendents of the Israelites, the chosen people of God. They believe that Jews, as the children of Satan, are behind everything that is wrong with America. They circulated a document proposing to kill all Jews and other nonwhites, whom they called "mud people" because they "lack souls."

Dr. Wesley Swift, a former Methodist minister turned bigot, anti-Semite, and anti-Catholic had founded the church, and when he died in 1970 Butler took over as leader of the racist movement. Three years later, he moved the sect to Hayden Lake, where he established a compound that included a plain home for himself, a church, a meeting hall, a printing business, a campground, and watch towers — a fortified headquarters for white supremacists. It became a meeting place for those of like views and a training centre for those waiting for the day when the whites would take over North America and drive out all other races. On paper, the organization is nonviolent, but events that occurred in July 1984, while Nerland was in Hayden Lake attending the Fifth Congress of Aryan Nations, were very violent and they were carried out by Butler's followers.

Two years before, Aryan Nations member Dan Bauer and visitor Bob Matthews met at Hayden Lake and became friends. By September 1983, they had founded the Silent Brotherhood and began a series of murders and robberies designed to rid the world of enemies of the supremacists and enhance the coffers of the Aryan Nations.

Matthews attended the shooting death of radio broadcaster Allen Berg, in Denver, Colorado, in June 1984. The popular Berg was guilty of being a Jew and criticizing the far right. A month later, while Nerland practiced hand-to-hand combat and killing techniques, Matthews and members of the brotherhood carried out the armed robbery of $3.6 million from a Brink's truck in Ukiah, California, and arrived back at Hayden Lake in time for Canadian member Edgar Foth to take his turn guarding the perimeter of the compound during the congress.

A few months after his training session at the Aryan Nations compound, Carney was invited to Louisiana by a man he had met at Hayden Lake, Karl Hand Jr., leader of the most violent of the right wing organizations. Hand was once the national organizer of the Ku Klux Klan for American presidential candidate David Duke. In 1984, he was leader of the National Socialist Liberation Front (NSLF) and Nerland was his captain in the Street Action branch of the NSLF, involved in violent confrontations with blacks and Jews whenever an opportunity arose.

It was during this period, in November 1985, that Nerland made his bizarre and unsuccessful attempt to enter Canada as American "Kurt Meyer." Nerland was a Canadian citizen, yet he used the name of a German general when being interviewed by a Canadian immigration officer at Calgary. Nerland gave a story that did not add up and carried business cards of weapons dealers and a photograph of himself in Nazi uniform bashing in the head of a mannequin, an exercise that was part of his Nazi training. He would clearly be barred from entry into the country. The story, as related by the immigration official at Nerland's bail hearing after Leo LaChance was shot, contributed to Nerland being denied bail. It seems to be the trip's only positive result.

Nerland visited Chile at various times during the 1980s, ostensibly carrying out his father's business concerns, and he married a Chilean woman. He also apparently took out Chilean citizenship and added Spanish to his self-taught German and his mother tongue which is English.

The marriage was unusual for a right-winger who espoused an all-white world, because his wife, Jacquie, is not totally Caucasian. A child, Stephanie, was born to the couple in 1989 after they settled in Prince Albert. After the shooting of Leo LaChance in January 1991, friends of Jacquie Nerland told police that Carney beat his wife and threatened to kill her if she attempted to leave him. Jacquie supplied her own sworn statement saying the allegations were false. Other friends say they were true. True or not, the marriage dissolved soon after Nerland was jailed for killing Leo LaChance.

In Prince Albert, Nerland had a variety of jobs, largely in sales, as a clothier, and as a door-to-door vacuum cleaner salesman. But what he really wanted to do was to own a gun shop, not an unusual ambition among white supremacists because it provides an armoury for their activities. In September 1989, when he became the Saskatchewan leader of the Church of Jesus Christ Christian Aryan Nations, he was working at a pawn shop just around the corner from the shop he later established in March of 1990.

Nerland believed himself to have a sense of humour, but those who witnessed his pranks found them far from funny. As a Halloween prank, he donned his Ku Klux Klan robes and put on a performance of racial slurs and jokes at a local bar. When a local man hesitated to fire a handgun in Nerland's store, Nerland demonstrated there was nothing to be afraid of by firing off several rounds into the floor.

When a Canadian war veteran displayed a Nazi flag on Hitler's birthday, in admiration of the dictator's prewar economic accomplishment, the story appeared in the Prince Albert *Daily Herald* and a small furor erupted. Nerland expressed his feelings of self-importance as an Aryan Nations leader when, under an assumed name, Nerland wrote a letter to the *Herald* editor defending the man's actions. When reporters called to ask about his leadership of the Aryan Nations, he replied with another threatening letter to the editor suggesting the paper was run by Jews.

There will always be a question as to what kind of organization Nerland was leading in Saskatchewan. The RCMP say there were at most six Aryan Nations followers in the entire province. Others claim there were plenty of sympathizers. Nerland tried to make the Aryan Nations a presence. He had a great deal of reading material and many opinions to share with anyone who asked. Even the occasional Indian, who certainly did not ask, got an earful anyway. His partner and his friends say he never tried to convert them, however.

Whether he had a following or not, in September 1990, Nerland, as head of the Saskatchewan branch was invited to attend an Aryan Nations Fest in Provost, Alberta. At that time, a uniformed city police constable was posing as a sympathizer to gather information about Nerland. When the police officer heard Nerland talk about the fest, he asked to go along. He was told he was welcome to go and would meet other police officers there. The constable did not go however, and, as it turned out, he could watch Nerland's behaviour from his own living room in Prince Albert. The Saskatchewan leader's aggressive behaviour drew national television coverage. Still, in Prince Albert, no one foresaw the tragedy he would soon inflict on the LaChance family.

On the weekend of the Aryan Nations Fest, thirty or forty white supremacists gathered on the farm of Ray Bradley, founder of the Brotherhood of Racial Purity. Nerland was in charge of security. As it was held on privately owned land, the event allowed Nerland to bring an array of weaponry for the boys to play with on the weekend, when they were not involved in cross lightings, bull sessions, or listening to inspirational taped messages by various supremacist leaders. School students in the small Alberta town had heard about the upcoming fest and protested by dressing in black a few days before it began. The rally drew a number of protestors. Nerland and the Aryan Nations delegates met them at the farm gate with their choice of weapons. Nerland favoured a pistol-handled shotgun.

Local residents contented themselves with standing back and watching. A few carried signs. Among those who had come some distance to protest were Harvey Kane, leader of the Jewish Defence League based in Calgary, and Sigmund Sobolewski, who is not Jewish but is a survivor of Auschwitz, a Second World War Nazi death camp. With them were a handful of reporters, photographers, and cameramen. The predictable happened. The two sides shouted remarks that soon provoked anger. Nerland's verbal attacks were particularly outrageous and vicious. Focusing on Sobolewski, he shouted, "Why don't you tell me they made fucking soap out of your auntie and fucking luggage out of your uncle. They made luggage out of him. I've got it in the fucking trunk of my car. I've got luggage made from your fucking uncle." Nerland also pointed the shotgun in Kane's direction and announced that the weapon was a form of birth control. "A 12-gauge shotgun cuts a person right in half; it's just great for preventing further Jewish births. It's a way to customize the womb."

When the weekend was over, Nerland returned to his small pawn and gun shop on River Street West in Prince Albert. The man who professed to hate Jews and Natives rented a store from a Jew and had a treaty Indian partner, Darwin Bear. It was business as usual. Gun buffs dropped in, looked around, chatted awhile, and bought or sold guns. An order of Ishapoor rifles, similar to the FNC-1 the Canadian military had used for thirty years, sold well. Police dropped by, both as customers and on their routine checks of all pawn stores, looking for items recently stolen and pawned.

Nerland entertained his friends and sometimes shocked them with his behaviour. Most customers knew it is illegal to fire weapons inside a store and refused to participate in Nerland's games. Nerland had no such qualms. More than once he demonstrated a weapon's capabilities by firing rounds into the floor. But unbelievably, with all the visiting that went on at the Northern Pawn and Gun Shop, his friends say Nerland never discussed his racist views with them. Even the night Leo LaChance was shot, conversation between Nerland and his two visitors, Gar Brownbridge and Russ Yungwirth, was said to be a two hour marathon discussion of the Gulf War only. It is hard to believe that Nerland's racist point of view apparently did not enter into the debate at all.

The antics at the Provost Aryan Nations Fest resulted in complaints to the Alberta government by those who were offended by what they saw on television and in the newspapers. An inquiry was held to look into the gathering at Provost, the actions of the Church of Jesus Christ Aryan Nations and its Canadian leader Terry Long, and the host for the fest, Ray Bradley, founder of the Brotherhood for Racial Purity (BHORP).

The inquiry, conducted by the Alberta Human Rights Commission in Edmonton, began 24 July 1991. Long defended himself. During the inquiry, he usually questioned Nerland first, then Bruce Mintz who was the lawyer for Harvey Kane, who had laid the complaints about the Aryan Nations Fest that led to the hearings. When Nerland appeared to testify, he seemed to understand Long well enough, but he expressed a sneering difficulty with questions posed by Mintz. Still, the picture of a true believer emerged. Yes, Carney Nerland, Prince Albert gun shop owner convicted of shooting Cree man Leo LaChance to death, was a member of the Church of Jesus Christ Christian Aryan Nations; he had been the Saskatchewan leader of the church since September 1989 and yes, he was a member of the Ku Klux Klan.

"The name Adolf Hitler, does that have any religious significance to you?" he was asked by Long. Nerland replied, "To me, personally, it does. Adolf Hitler, as far as I am concerned from my research and what I have read in the Bible, I would consider Adolf Hitler to be Elijah the Prophet, the prophet sent forth by God in the last days." Nerland denied that the Holocaust had occurred: "I personally feel it is the biggest misshapen misrepresented sickish joke of the twentieth century," he told the inquiry. "I don't believe it occurred in any way shape or form as they present it."

"I am not ashamed of my racial background," Nerland continued. "I believe that the white Aryan peoples of Western Europe are the most gifted people on earth, that they have enlightened the world in their culture and their technological advances, and I feel no shame just saying that I'm proud to be white, and I make no apologies whatsoever." Although later he would claim he had no dislike of Indians and point to the fact he had a treaty Indian partner, his view was a bit different at the Alberta inquiry: "No, I don't hate Indians. I hate many of the things they do, I hate, I hate the way that they felt that they should be treated better than average Canadians. I do not believe they want equality, they want more than equality. They want to be treated better than everyone else." He also told the Alberta inquiry that he did not hate Blacks generally, "only those that are opposed to the interests of whites, communist Negroes, terrorist Negroes, AIDS-carrying Negroes, homosexual Negroes, pedophile Negroes, sodomite Negroes, but not Negroes in general. As a whole race, I am sure there are a few and some of them could be described as good."

Nerland told the Alberta inquiry he had taken the weapons to Provost to keep infiltrators and unwanted people away. The weapons were loaded because an unloaded gun is absolutely useless, he said.

In their conclusions, the inquiry commissioners said, "The Aryan Nations Fest was a shocking event in the history of Alberta. The blatant display of signs and symbols redolent of racial and religious hatred, bigotry and discrimination challenge the very foundations of our society." They said there was no doubt about the hatred Terry Long and Carney Nerland felt for Jews, native Canadians, and nonwhites. "We have no doubt about the lengths they would be prepared to go, given the opportunity, to implement their evil plans. The hatred in the court was palpable. It was patently clear these are not simply misguided eccentrics. They are dedicated Nazis."

It was four months after the Aryan Nations Fest in Provost that Carney Nerland shot and killed Leo LaChance.

CHAPTER TWELVE

The Police

28 January 1991

As constables Ian Reiman and Troy Cooper followed the ambulance to the Holy Family Hospital, Reiman alerted his shift sergeant, Wilf Savisky, that a crime had been committed. Sergeant Savisky immediately dispatched two police officers to guard the scene and telephoned Staff Sergeant Dave Demkiw, head of the Prince Albert Police Criminal Investigations Branch, who was at home relaxing after dinner. Demkiw pulled on a jacket and headed back to the office. Detective sergeants Gerry Novotny and Peter Mesluk were also called in. They were to be the main investigators in the case.

All but Mesluk are members of the old school of Canadian police officers. They are all big men, big enough to settle some disputes merely by their presence. There is not much they have not seen happen and there is not much police work that ruffles them. Many have more than twenty years behind their badges. The people they have dealt with respect them, often even like them. They are good cops. They know police work is not very exciting and that the solutions may not please the public, but they know how to solve a crime if it can be solved and they do it by the book.

Detective Sergeant Peter Mesluk, thirty-three at the time, had been a police officer for fourteen years, ten of those years as a sergeant with the Prince Albert Police Department. He grew up in Prince Albert, on the grounds of the tuberculosis sanatorium north of the river where his father was a food services manager. Peter is one of the newer breed of police officer. He looks smaller, more compact, in excellent physical condition. In civilian clothes, he does not look like a cop. He has a quiet, shy manner that belies a sharp insightful mind that misses nothing. Mesluk is also a family man. He does not drink or smoke. He had to have a vice, he jokes, so he owns a racehorse.

His partner, Detective Sergeant Gerry Novotny, then forty-five, is a tall, soft-spoken man, a veteran police officer and a hometown boy well-known for his involvement in youth sports and his enthusiasm for golf. Persons talking to Sergeant Novotny know they have his complete attention and concern for whatever they have to say. Around the office, he is a good-natured prankster.

Mesluk was about to relax in front of the television set when the call about the shooting on River Street came. He had worked late that day and had just finished supper. He noted the time in his notebook: 7:08 P.M. Twelve minutes later, he met with Demkiw, Novotny, and Savisky in Demkiw's office. Mesluk and Novotny were told they would handle the investigation.

At that moment, there was very little information available. Savisky told the investigators a 911 call had been received at 6:34 P.M. Constables Troy Cooper and Ian Reiman and a Parkland ambulance had been dispatched to the 100 block of River Street West. An unidentified man had been found collapsed on the sidewalk in front of Hewitt's Auction. One man had spoken Cree to the fallen man. A second passerby had provided a blanket and a third man had run several blocks to telephone for help. When the paramedics examined the victim, they found he had been either shot or stabbed. He was at the Holy Family Hospital, being prepared for the trip to Saskatoon where he would undergo emergency surgery. Constables Cooper and Reiman were with him at the hospital.

They had identified the victim as Leo LaChance, sometimes known as Leo Roberts, a forty-eight-year-old man from the Big River Reserve near Debden. Demkiw sent Novotny and Mesluk to the scene and then he hurried to the hospital from where he would coordinate the investigation.

Novotny and Mesluk were at the scene by 7:30 P.M. Two police constables had been there since 7 P.M. to take notes and to protect whatever evidence there might be. There was not much to see. The only obvious clues were imprints in the snow and a spot of saliva. A police officer was sent to the hospital to fetch LaChance's boots; it was hoped they would match some of the footprints in the area. The investigators would then have an idea of LaChance's movements before he was shot.

Paramedics Bellisle and Ferland, having delivered LaChance to hospital, returned to the scene of the shooting, but they were unable to add much. Mesluk asked them to prepare a statement and drop it off at the police station later. Finally, at 7:40 P.M., a message from the hospital was relayed to the officers at the scene. Cooper had learned this much from the wounded man: Leo LaChance had had an argument with three men at Katz's and "a gun accidentally went off."

Savisky sent for the owner of Katz Bros. Hide and Fur store. Ninety-year-old Arnold Katz arrived and let police into his building. He was fully prepared to cooperate but he had little to offer. He had closed up shop at 5:30 P.M. and he had not seen Leo LaChance at all that day.

Meanwhile Leo's Kamik boots had been brought to the scene. They fit the footprints leading to the door of Katz Bros. Hide and Fur Shop adjoining the Northern Pawn and Gun Shop perfectly.

Katz Bros. Fur and Hide has been located in the same place since 1926. Arnold Katz and his brother, the late Harold Katz, had the double store built to accommodate their growing enterprise in the heydey of the trade. Now Arnold's fur and hide business occupies the east half of the building, while the west half has been rented to a succession of entrepreneurs over the years, including Carney Nerland and Darwin Bear, who in March 1990, opened the Northern Pawn and Gun Shop.

Inside Katz's store, facing the main entrance, there is a door that leads to the basement. As he stepped inside, Sergeant Mesluk noticed greasy-looking footprints leading to the basement, perhaps made by a repairman who had been working there that afternoon.

There was a partially open door leading to the other half of the basement, the portion under Nerland's gun shop. As the detectives walked through the doorway Mesluk thought he had come across a "mini range" — a wooden pallet leaning against a basement wall had been used as a target backstop. The floor was littered with spent cartridge casings and there were hundreds of bullet holes everywhere.

A stairway was located at the left side of the basement. "We could see light coming through. The door looked to be ajar. We forced the door open and went up into Nerland's store. We made a cursory search," Mesluk would later say. In fact, they were looking to see if there were any other shooting victims. "We took one or two photos. We were unsure of our ground — being in there. I wasn't sure it was legal. We were walking on eggshells. We were in there two minutes tops." Now they were determined to search the pawn and gun shop as quickly as they could obtain permission from the owners.

Outside, the police detectives continued to look for clues. It was very cold and dark; the neighbourhood was deserted. They searched through the empty lot beside the building and along the laneway leading to parking lots and back doors of businesses shut tight for the night.

As Mesluk and Novotny walked along River Street toward the bridge, they passed in front of Katz Bros. Fur and Hide store, the Northern Pawn and Gun Shop, and a karate school, which was located on the corner of the one-lane street, Second Avenue West, immediately across from the high concrete side of the John Diefenbaker Bridge. There, the two detectives found what they were looking for — footprints made by LaChance's boots. One was located in front of the karate school, and another at the base of the steps down from the bridge. They followed the trail across the bridge to the northwest side and off the walkway. It looked as if someone had urinated in the snow. It appeared a vehicle had dropped a passenger off there. The two detectives walked back across the bridge to the shops on River Street. Shortly after 9 P.M. they returned to the station.

Sergeant Savisky found the names and home telephone numbers of the gun shop's two owners on their license applications and called both immediately. Darwin Bear lived on the Little Red Reserve, eighty kilometres north of town, but he promised to report to the police station as soon as possible. Nerland could not be reached at his home. The investigators did not know he and his family were enjoying a family supper at sister Hali's home.

Meanwhile, at the police station, the first witness on the scene, Kim Koroll, told police that he went into the gunshop to telephone for help. There he encountered three men, all of them white. One had a beard. He believed it was the man behind the counter who said there was no telephone in the shop.

At 10:30 P.M., Darwin Bear, a slight, quiet young man, arrived at the police station. He was told there had been a shooting on River Street around 6:30 that evening. Police wanted to search the pawn and gun shop he co-owned with Carney Nerland. Bear readily agreed and at 10:47 P.M., he signed a consent to search form. Bear told police that, as far as he knew, Nerland was having dinner with his father. He had not seen his partner since earlier that afternoon.

Sergeant Mesluk, a careful investigator, was still uncomfortable about the legalities of searching the store without permission from both owners and was unwilling to lose a case in court on a technicality. He talked to Staff Sergeant Demkiw and then began to draft a search warrant based on the information police had obtained.

While Nerland dined with his family, Leo LaChance was the subject of much attention at the Holy Family Hospital. The emergency team was working to stabilize his deteriorating condition. Constables Reiman and Cooper were now on duty at the hospital. Reiman had been collecting LaChance's clothing as the doctors removed it. He had placed each piece in a sealed plastic bag and those he promptly delivered to Corporal Parker, in the police identification section, who locked them away. Parker itemized the clothing for the RCMP Forensic Laboratory in Regina: "one blue jacket . . . possible bullet holes left arm and left armpit area; one red sweater . . . possible bullet holes, left arm and left armpit area; one purple shirt . . . possible bullet holes, left arm and left armpit area."

Constable Cooper had waited more than an hour after the ambulance arrived at the hospital for his chance to question LaChance. It was a stroke of luck that Cooper had been one of the first officers to respond to the call. He had grown up in the town of Big River, a few miles from the reserve, and he could understand Cree well enough to interview LaChance in either that language or English.

LaChance was in great pain. He tried to talk to Cooper, but he could hardly say the words. When he did manage, he spoke only English. Cooper asked Leo what had happened to him. He gasped, "They shot me!" LaChance told Cooper what he could in short, badly garbled bursts of sound. The story LaChance managed to tell was that three white men with rifles had shot him inside Katz's fur shop. He said he had gone into the store to try to sell his furs but the white men did not want to buy them. There was no argument. They shot him, but it must have been an accident.

Doctors were preparing LaChance for the trip to the Royal University Hospital, 140 kilometres away in Saskatoon. His blood pressure was dropping and he was in a great deal of pain. Cooper planned to accompany LaChance in the ambulance to Saskatoon where he would have a further opportunity to question LaChance on the way. The officer realized the importance of a dying declaration and knew it needed to be verbatim, but getting any kind of a statement was proving to be a struggle. Parkland Ambulance arrived to transport LaChance to Saskatoon. Through an oversight, no police officer accompanied LaChance. Constables Cooper and Reiman returned to the station to make their reports.

LaChance seemed to be trying to put Cooper off, to shut him up so that Leo could concentrate on his own problems. He did not give the impression that he thought he might die. He asked that police contact his brother David, or his sister Roseanne. There did not seem to be more he could add to what he had already managed to tell Cooper.

At the Royal University Hospital, two Saskatoon police officers were waiting for Leo LaChance. Between them, sergeants Terry Cline and Ed Koolick had more than fifty years of experience gathering information from seriously wounded people. They knew the LaChance interview was not going to be easy.

The Parkland ambulance swung into the receiving area of the emergency wing at 9:40 P.M. A medical team was standing by. Cline and Koolick had very little time to act. As LaChance was wheeled to the observation room, Cline asked, "Who did this to you?" LaChance replied, "I don't know."

Doctor Dale Ardell, who had accompanied LaChance in the ambulance, told the police that he had asked the wounded man several times in the ambulance on the trip from Prince Albert and the reply had always been the same: "I don't know."

Over the next hour, Cline persisted whenever he could get near enough to LaChance to pose a question. The task was difficult for everyone involved since a medical team was preparing LaChance for surgery. Both police and doctors were working in a tiny observation room, trying to cooperate with each other as best they could.

LaChance was in obvious pain. Although he remained conscious and answered questions for medical and police teams, he frequently broke off in midanswer to moan or writhe about. Cline managed about ten minutes of questioning over the hour, and most of that just before LaChance was wheeled into the operating room.

LaChance told the police officer he had been down on River Street hoping to sell furs at a place Cline understood to be "Gates." He said he went into the store where he thought "Gates" lived and was met by "three white guys." He kept telling Cline there were three white guys. One had a rifle, and the one with a rifle shot him.

Moments later, LaChance was wheeled into surgery. Cline had time only for a hurried telephone call to Prince Albert police to report what he had learned and then he too entered the operating room. If the bullet was successfully removed, Cline would be there to receive it for evidence.

Within five hours after LaChance had been found, the police

had traced his movements before and after he was shot. But they still did not know where, how, or why the shooting had occurred. They had only what he had been able to tell them: he had been in Katz's fur shop with three white men. According to Leo, the men had not said anything to him nor had they asked him to leave. He asked if they were interested in buying his furs. They said no. A tall white man about forty shot him, and after he was shot he left the store.

This was all the information the investigators had when Carney Nerland finally appeared at the police station. It was 11:43 P.M.

Sergeants Mesluk and Novotny told Nerland that a search warrant was being prepared and his partner had already been contacted. Whether Nerland agreed or not, police would search the store and among the evidence they would be looking for would be blood stains to indicate whether anyone had been shot in the store. The detectives wanted Nerland to be fully aware that any game playing he might indulge in would not in any way hinder their search. They told Nerland that Kim Koroll had said that he had gone into the gun and pawn shop, asked to use the telephone to call 911, and had been refused. Koroll had told police three men had been in the store at the time, one of them was bearded.

Nerland leaned back in his chair and replied, "I think I can help you guys." But first, he wanted to know what would happen if an accidental shooting had in fact occurred. "What would a guy get or be charged with?" he asked the two detectives. At that point, the police did not yet know they were dealing with a murder case. LaChance was in hospital in Saskatoon. There had been no word.

Sergeant Novotny left the interview room and returned with a copy of the Criminal Code of Canada. He showed Nerland the possible charges: pointing a firearm, possession of a firearm, discharging a firearm, and so on. What interested Mesluk was that Nerland promptly read the whole section in detail. He was not stalling, he seemed genuinely interested. The explanations of summary (less serious) and indictable (serious) charges caught his eye. He wanted to know what they meant.

"What would happen to me if someone shot a gun on my premises?" he wanted to know. "That would depend on the circumstances," he was told. The prosecutor would make the final decision.

Nerland confided that something had indeed happened in his shop that night. He was going to tell the police all about it but he was scared of the guys he was going to talk about and he was afraid for his family. He indicated that someone else had done the shooting. He was told that if someone else had discharged a firearm in his store, he could be charged with unsafe storage of a weapon. With that, Nerland began his statement:

> I am part owner in Northern Pawn and Gun. With a Darwin Bear. On January 28th, 1991, I opened the store by 11:00 A.M. I continued business until around 6:00 P.M., when I started to gear down to close-up. I was a little bit later because I was cleaning up and doing paper work. I was putting stuff away and a couple of gentlemen came in. They were in their late 20's. I really didn't feel awfully comfortable with them there, there was 2 of them, I was hoping they would get the hint to leave, and I continued working. What I mean, is I'm putting guns away in my safe in a gun locker, I'm taking guns off the display board and I'm putting them in the safe. I've got my back to these guys and I'm hoping they leave, all the while they're touching things, and handling weapons. The one wearing the dark coat picked up, well I didn't see what he had picked up as my back was turned as I was putting things away. It was at this time I heard a shot go off. I didn't hear any screams or glass break. I turned around and this guy had a dumb look on his face and he passes the gun an M-56 to me and smiles over at his friend. I took the gun and removed the magazine, placed the gun in the gun closet and I put the clip on the counter. I would think the casing is on the floor somewhere. This gun is actually a folding stock rifle, and shoots a 7.62 mm shell [pistol shell]. At this point I'm traumatized, I didn't know what I said, there were no other persons in the store. Just me and these two guys. I don't recall an Indian being in the store after 6:00 P.M.

The only other person that came in was a fellow that wanted to borrow the phone. He had wondered if there was a phone he could use. And he had stated something to the effect that someone had fallen on the ice. I wanted to get out of this situation, I just told him "no". Well, I just shook my head "No." He left. Then the guy looked at me and said "Keep your fucking mouth shut." This was the guy that had shot the gun wearing the dark jacket. The two guys shuffled off and I quickly finished my business, set my alarm and closed. I just wanted to get out of there.

Mesluk and Novotny began to question Nerland for further details:

Q. What more can you tell us about these two guys?

A. One guy had a red jacket, midlength past his waist, average length hair, under two hundred pounds, collar length. The guy with the darker jacket, midlength, under two hundred pounds, brown hair, shorter hair cut.

Q. These two were unknown to you, right?

A. Yes.

Q. Where do you keep the ammunition?

A. I keep it either on the counter or in the case.

Q. What about this particular 7.62 mm ammo?

A. I must have ten boxes of it, and in close proximity. I have some spare magazines, and they, I believe, one of them was loaded, it wouldn't have had more than one shell in it. This is what I think might have happened. It's the only explanation I can think of. The guy saw a clip and put it in, like I said these guys were picking things up as I was trying to put them away.

Q. Can we go to your store and get the gun?

A. Yes, you can.

Q. How many 7.62 guns do you have?

A. Just the one.

"I feel like a victim," Nerland commented when he finished his statement. It was 1:06 A.M. He said again he wanted to cooperate with police. "I didn't have anything to do with it." He signed the consent form to have the store searched. It was then 1:11 A.M. Carney Nerland, Darwin Bear, and sergeants Mesluk and Novotny headed for the car park.

Once inside the store, Novotny walked to the spot where Nerland had said the two strangers had stood. He looked at the door to the street and spotted a tiny hole in the flag draped across the glass. Examining it more closely, Novotny concluded the bullet that made the hole in the flag had penetrated the door frame. The bullet hole was fresh. It was the first indication the shooting might have occurred inside the store.

Novotny put a metal probe into the hole in the door frame to get an indication of the trajectory of the shot. The two detectives exchanged glances. Something was not right here.

The bullet had not come from where Nerland had said the two strangers had stood. It had come from behind the counter. Nerland had noticed that glance too.

The two detectives said nothing. The identification officer, Corporal Parker, was gathering evidence and taking photographs. There were three drinking glasses on the counter that smelled of rye and cola. The officers noticed bullet holes in the floor, the wall, and the heating vent, but the holes were not considered important evidence at that point.

When the police asked for the gun, Nerland told them it was in the green gun safe, or locker, behind the counter. They wanted to open it right there but Nerland claimed he did not have the key with him. He told them it contained some personal papers, firearms, and jewelry. When the police announced they would take the whole gun safe to the police station, Nerland seemed surprised. He blustered about a receipt and was given one by Mesluk, who found his behaviour odd. "He'd been really good up until then. I don't know why he'd want a receipt. I think he was a little taken aback that we would want to take the safe as well."

Novotny and Mesluk took Bear and Nerland back to the police station with them. The two shop owners were asked to wait in the front office while the detectives conferred. The police had a good idea about what had happened at the gun shop that night, but they did not have enough evidence to hold Bear or Nerland. The two men were released at 3:10 A.M.

The detectives then went home to sleep before the 7 A.M. start of their regular day. But Bear and Nerland went back to the pawn and gun shop. Nerland wanted police to believe he was such a law-abiding man that he was worried he had broken the law that required burglar alarms in all gun shops. He had not reactivated his. He did not hurry, however. Nerland and Bear left the police station at 3:10 A.M. but did not arrive at the gun shop, only eight blocks away, for fifty minutes. When they finally got to the shop, they found Constable Boyd Prodaehl on duty and they told him they must set the alarm. Prodaehl told them it would not be necessary since the store would be under constant police guard. They persisted and Prodaehl eventually let them into the shop. Now it became clear why they had been so persistent. Nerland wanted to take a ledger home with him but the police officer refused to even consider it. Nerland continued to argue, however, and finally, a compromise was reached. The ledger was put in a briefcase and locked in the gun locker. The two men left the officer to his vigil. Prodaehl filed a report on the incident but it was not passed on to the chief investigators right away so they had no idea of Nerland's early morning antics with the ledger in the briefcase until a few days later.

⚬ ⚬

In Saskatoon, Sergeant Terry Cline took his notebook out of his pocket and dialled the number of the Prince Albert Police Department. The operating room staff was cleaning up and preparing the area for the next emergency surgery. Orderlies were wheeling Leo LaChance downstairs.

"He didn't make it," Cline reported.

Cline had not thought Leo would survive but the medical staff had made every attempt. Shortly after 10:30 P.M., surgeons had begun the seemingly hopeless task of repairing the damage the bullet had done. Tearing through Leo's left arm, it had entered his chest and drilled a tunnel through his diaphragm, arteries, spleen, gall bladder, liver, a rib on his right side, and finally slowed to a stop, buried in the muscle layer near the skin. The doctors left it there for the pathologist to remove during the autopsy the next morning. They had done what they could. They had repaired torn blood vessels and removed an amazing amount of blood from the abdominal cavity. The patient had received more than thirty pints of blood and the best that the surgeons could do for him. But at fifty-five minutes after midnight, 29 January 1991, Leo LaChance died and all their efforts would not bring him back to life.

CHAPTER THIRTEEN

The Arrest

29 January 1991

Prince Albert

On Tuesday morning, just five hours after they had left the Northern Pawn and Gun Shop, detectives Gerry Novotny and Peter Mesluk were back at the Prince Albert police station.

An unexpected lead came from Sergeant Gary Drake who heard that the two detectives were looking for a bearded man. Drake was police office manager and firearms registrar. He remembered Roy McKnight, who had recently applied for a permit to become a partner in the Northern Pawn and Gun Shop. Drake knew McKnight was a large man with a full beard and thought he was a possibility. He took the application to Novotny and Mesluk early Tuesday morning. The detectives drove to McKnight's house, but he was not there, so the detectives left their names and number.

Back in their car, they received a message for them on the radio that Bob Nerland, Carney's father, was waiting for them at the gun shop. They picked him up and took him to the police station to take a statement. They had known Big Bob, as he was called, from the days when he lived and worked in Prince Albert. Big Bob had little to add.

He had been at the store Monday afternoon and he and Carney had gone to the Marlboro Inn to eat. Bob left around 4 P.M., he said, and saw Carney again that evening at seven when the family gathered at his daughter Hali's for dinner. According to Bob, Carney ate well. He said nothing at all about any incident. Nor did he mention a word about the shooting to his father when they met the following morning.

The elder Nerland refused to sign his statement until he had reviewed it with his lawyer in Regina. He gave a Regina address as his home, corroborated by a Saskatchewan driver's license. However, he had no intention of going to Regina that day. He planned to leave that afternoon, 29 January, for Alberta where, unknown to police, he really lived.

Nerland's sister, Hali, noted in her statement that Carney had not been himself that evening at her dinner party but their brother, Alfin, was there and she thought Carney's moodiness was because of a fight he had had with him a few days earlier. When she was told the day after her party that the police were looking for her father and brother in connection with a shooting on River Street, Hali simply did not believe her father and brother would have reason to be involved.

At 1:20 P.M. of 29 January, Carney Nerland called police to tell them he planned to go to Alberta that day with his father to buy a van. The call came as a surprise. Mesluk and Novotny did not like the idea of Nerland leaving the province but there was nothing they could do about it.

A few minutes later, Roy McKnight, the man with the beard, arrived at the police station to talk to the two detectives. But clearly he did not like being there and he was not overly cooperative. Still, he gave a statement. McKnight told police he had been in the shop at approximately 5:15 P.M. the day of the shooting. He had a quick drink, talked about the Gulf War for awhile and then called his wife to find out when supper was. She had told him "ten minutes ago," so he quickly left for home. At approximately 10:30 P.M. that night, Nerland visited McKnight and asked him to go for a drive. He needed advice. What would happen if police found out weapons had been fired in the shop? McKnight put it bluntly: "Your ass is grass." McKnight insisted Nerland had mentioned not a word about an individual — or Leo LaChance

— being shot and killed. The two had parted just before midnight. Novotny and Mesluk had the clear impression he was hiding something.

The interview with McKnight was interrupted by two telephone calls. The first was from Big Bob Nerland who demanded to know why the RCMP highway patrol cars were on the lookout for him. He had been stopped as he left town and told that the city police wanted to talk to him. Mesluk promised to tell the Mounties that Big Bob had already been interviewed. The second call came half an hour after the Nerlands left town. It was from Balicki, Popescul and Company, a Prince Albert law firm that was acting for Russell Yungwirth and Gar Brownbridge. The two men had witnessed the shooting and were prepared to talk to police in the company of their lawyers.

Yungwirth and and Brownbridge told police they had been with Carney Nerland in his gunshop the previous evening when an elderly, intoxicated Indian had wandered into the store wanting to sell a .303 rifle. Nerland had not talked to the man but he had fired two shots into the floor from a weapon he had in his hands. When the Indian looked disgusted and left, a third shot was fired. The two friends said Nerland looked shocked and muttered about not knowing there was a third bullet in the rifle, which he had pointed and fired as the door closed.

The statements of Yungwirth, Brownbridge, and Carney Nerland have interesting similarities: there are two people in the store with Nerland; a shot is fired toward the door; the person firing the gun has a "surprised," "stunned," or "dumb" look on his face; a man walks in and asks for the telephone because someone is "laying on the sidewalk" — "passed out on the sidewalk" or has "slipped on the ice," all innocuous reasons that do not suggest serious harm or imminent danger.

All set the scene for manslaughter, not murder. To lay a charge of murder in Canada, prosecutors must prove, beyond a reasonable doubt, that the killer intended to murder the victim. When Yungwirth and Brownbridge both claimed that Nerland was surprised by the last shot, they effectively freed Carney Nerland from being convicted of murder. Clearly a judge or jury could not be convinced beyond a reasonable doubt that the shooting was planned and intentional.

After Yungwirth and Brownbridge gave their statements, Mesluk and Novotny returned to the gun shop. There were the two fresh holes in the floor, giving credence to Yungwirth and Brownbridge's story that Nerland had first fired two shots into the floor before firing in LaChance's direction as he left the shop. While they were there, they made an inventory of the weapons still in the store. There were thirty-nine rifles on the walls, fifteen rifles in pawn, and sixteen handguns on display.

The following day, the detectives were scheduled to meet with John Field, a highly regarded crown prosecutor in Saskatchewan for fourteen years. In his forties, Field is a slight, scholarly-looking man with a bushy moustache. He has a Master's degree in Law from the University of London, England. He was given the entire LaChance file, containing everything the police knew to that point in the investigation. RCMP eventually provided much more information about Nerland's Aryan Nations connections at Hayden Lake, Idaho, and in Louisiana. Now he had to decide what charge should be laid.

Even though Nerland was not yet facing charges, there had been two calls to Crime Stoppers warning that Nerland was probably going to flee the country. Those calls formed the basis of Field's first question: Is Nerland likely to flee the country and perhaps go to South America? He had spent some time in Chile and had married a Chilean woman. If so, a charge of manslaughter would be drawn up immediately and a Canada-wide warrant issued.

Field was bothered by the fact that Yungwirth and Brownbridge said they had seen nothing on River Street as they hurried from the gun shop shortly after the shooting. That did not fit with the fact that the ambulance arrived within a few minutes of the 911 call and the police report that no car was parked in front of the gunshop when they arrived a minute later. Leo LaChance must have been visible to them. Field asked the police to find out if the ambulance had used flashing lights and a siren. There were lights. No siren.

His next question dealt with the same concern: Can you see the spot where Leo fell from Nerland's store? Mesluk wrote in the margin, "Yes, fifty yards max."

Field told Mesluk and Novotny to get a statement from Arnold Katz on any shots fired that day when he was at his store. Mesluk said Katz refused to give a statement. Mesluk was not surprised that an elderly man would hesitate to become involved in something he could not hope to change.

The prosecutor wanted to know if Leo LaChance had known he was close to death and he asked for a detailed statement from the Saskatoon police officers who interviewed him. Leo's understanding of whether or not he might die would have an impact on the court's assessment of what he had told police. If a person believes he is dying, his statements are believed to be factual because he has nothing to gain at that point by lying.

The prosecutor listed several other important tasks he wanted the detectives to do. The door of the gun shop was to be seized for evidence. Instead, the critical section with the bullet hole was removed that day and sent to the forensic laboratory in Regina. Roy McKnight was to be interviewed again about the conversation he had had with Nerland when they had gone for their drive the night of the shooting and the following morning when they had met for coffee. (Mesluk later testified that this was not done. McKnight clearly did not want to talk and was unlikely to add anything to what he had already said.) Statements were to be gathered from everyone at the scene; the two detectives were able to report that this had already been completed.

The prosecutor was curious to know why Darwin Bear and Nerland had returned to the store at 3 A.M. Tuesday morning. Bear had insisted that they had wanted to see the business and gun registry ledgers, that was all. Mesluk told Field he knew no reason why Bear would lie.

Field was also interested in Leo LaChance's activities the day he had been shot, and so the investigators were to interview Morris Morin, the relative who had stopped to help the dying man.

Field had already concluded that manslaughter was the appropriate charge. Brownbridge and Yungwirth were the Crown's chief witnesses. Everything hinged on their statements to the police that Nerland did not know there was a third bullet in the gun. Therefore there were no grounds for laying a murder charge. Novotny drafted the information necessary for a justice of the peace to sign and the wording of the Canada-wide warrant. The charge of manslaughter was laid 30 January, within forty-eight hours after Leo had entered Nerland's gunshop.

Events moved very rapidly then. The warrant was put on the Canadian Police Information Centre computer system at 4:15 P.M. One minute later, the RCMP headquarters at Red Deer, Alberta, requested a description of Nerland. It was sent at 4:19 P.M. and relayed to the RCMP detachment at Coronation, Alberta. Ten minutes later, Mounties from Coronation had Nerland in custody and were headed toward the Saskatchewan border with their prisoner. Two Prince Albert city police officers immediately set out for Lloydminster, a city that straddles the Saskatchewan-Alberta border where at 10 P.M., they took Nerland into their custody. They then began the three-hundred-kilometre drive back to Prince Albert.

On 31 January, Mesluk and Novotny waited patiently until Nerland had finished his breakfast in the police cell before trying to talk to him. This was a very different Nerland from the man they had interviewed previously. He told them he was not intimidated or afraid of them. "I'm no fourteen-year-old-punk," he informed them. Nerland called Kevin Glass, a paralegal with the Legal Aid office in Prince Albert, a provincially supported service for those who cannot afford a private lawyer.

Sergeant Mesluk then read Nerland his rights: "You need not say anything. You have nothing to hope from any promise of favour and nothing to fear from any threat, whether or not you say anything. Anything you do say may be used as evidence. Do you understand?"

Nerland understood. He crossed his arms and looked at the detectives. "We just want your side of the story," Mesluk told him but the burly man just shrugged his shoulders. "I can't guarantee I am going to talk to police," he said.

Nerland then showed a surprising awareness of legal procedure. He told them he knew he would be remanded, held in custody at the provincial jail, until his hearing the following Monday and he knew there would be a bail hearing, steps in the criminal justice system of which first timers are not always aware. He bragged that going to jail did not upset him because many jail guards were friends of his. Then he sat back and laughed at them. "You have facts enough for a manslaughter charge and there's no point in me saying anything more until I talk with my lawyer," he said. Mesluk noted that although Nerland was cool and calculating, he was cooperative in answering questions even with his new "can't push me around" pose.

Meanwhile, Corporal Andy Lawrence from the National Crime Index Service in Regina called Sergeant Mesluk. He was concerned Nerland might flee the country if he was freed on bail because Nerland was a Chilean citizen and had a Chilean passport.

Corporal Lawrence met with the prosecutor and the two detectives 1 February. He supplied information and the names of people who would provide more — all designed to keep Nerland from being freed on bail. He also revealed the name of an RCMP informant on Aryan Nations activity in Prince Albert; information that was devastating for their case. It was going to bring everything the police said and did into question from then on. The bail hearing was set for Monday, 5 February 1991.

CHAPTER FOURTEEN

The Silence

Leo's body was returned to the reserve where he had been born and to the church where he had been baptised. His brother David LaChance supervised his funeral as he would his two sons' funerals, both dead within three years.

In the Big River Reserve Sacred Heart Mission Roman Catholic church the men sit on the right and the women on the left. There is a small raised chancel with a plain wooden lectern on the right. To the left is an electric organ facing the congregation. Three or four women sit in a semicircle in the outside aisle near the organ. They are the choir, and with Sister Angelle leading and playing the organ, they sing the hymns in Cree.

On the day of Leo's funeral, the central doors at the back opened and six family members and friends carried the coffin to the front. David and the rest of the LaChance relatives filed in and took their places in the front pews. The priest entered and the funeral service and Mass, conducted in English, began, interspersed with hymns sung softly in Cree.

After the Benediction, the coffin was carried outside and loaded back into the hearse. The wind was up a bit, but the temperature was rising steadily, as if in sympathy with the mourners. The congregation got into cars and trucks filling the snowy parking lot, drove a short way down the road, then turned to bump along a trail leading to a clearing in the bush and the Roman Catholic cemetery. After the priest said the interment prayers, the family put the first few shovelfulls of earth on the casket. Then, one by one, friends took a handful of dirt and silently said their last goodbyes.

Tragedy was no stranger to the LaChance family. They had not been able to bury Leo's brother, Samerie, or their sister, Virginia. Their bodies had never been returned to the Big River Reserve. There had been no comforting words and rites in their case — no peace to soften their loss — in fact there are still no answers as to why they died.

David has a few precious family photographs. One shows a pretty teenager, wearing shorts and a blouse, her head tilted to one side. That is Virginia, only seventeen when she died. One day in 1967, after she and her parents had gone to Taber, Alberta, to work in the sugar beet fields, she disappeared. Several days later, her body was found in a ditch. She had been stabbed to death. Her shattered parents identified her remains and left word with the priests and nuns on where they could be reached. They immediately went home to make the funeral arrangements. But Virginia was never returned to the Big River Reserve. For reasons that are unclear, Indian Affairs arranged for Virginia to be buried on a reserve near Taber, far from her family. The family was not informed and so were not present at her funeral. David thinks maybe it was too expensive to send her body home.

For years, he tried to find out who had murdered Virginia. He telephoned the RCMP at Taber regularly but he was always informed that the killer had not been found. Finally, he stopped calling. To this date, RCMP say they are unable to release any information because the case is still open.

Samerie LaChance had moved to Lethbridge, Alberta, where he worked and was raising a young family. At midnight, 17 July 1975, he was apparently walking home, along Highway 3 West, one kilometre past the Old Man River bridge. He climbed up out of a ditch and walked into the path of a car. He was struck and died instantly. The driver was not charged since it was considered to be an accident. Samerie had been drinking and his blood alcohol level was quite high.

His wife and six young children were left nearly destitute, with no idea of what assistance was available to them. Desperately in need of help, they called David LaChance. He and and his wife, Madeline, loaded their truck with food and clothing and left immediately for Alberta. David tried to find out what had happened exactly but he was never told, only that there was nothing unusual about the case.

Then their father's younger brother, Sam LaChance, disappeared. Sam was working in the bush near La Ronge in the 1980s, and frequently returned home to Prince Albert on weekends. He was last seen alive one summer evening walking along River Street West, not far from where Leo was shot. After that, he simply disappeared. Two friends were said to have witnessed an attack on Sam but they fled the city and never returned. Since there were no single clues to indicate anything unusual about the disappearance, the city police did not investigate it as a criminal case. They believe Sam went away for his own reasons, and did not bother to tell anyone. David maintains Sam would not do that to the family. He would have told them where he was going or gotten in touch somehow. The family believe he was murdered in Prince Albert and his body hidden somewhere in the bush.

This time, surely, there would be some answers. David was determined that questions about Leo's death would be answered. But it would not be easy. David heard on the radio that witnesses had already been found and an arrest made. No one told him when the bail hearing would be held.

On the earliest possible date after Nerland's arrest on 1 February, Nerland made his first appearance in provincial court. He entered no plea and had nothing to say. A bail hearing was arranged to determine if he would be released while awaiting trial. Meanwhile, he was taken back to the remand cells of the Prince Albert Correctional Centre, the provincial jail.

The bail hearing was held Monday, 5 February, in provincial courtroom one on the third floor of the McIntosh Mall, two blocks along River Street from the Northern Pawn and Gun Shop where Leo was killed. Along the north wall of the courtroom is a glassed-in dock with a row of paired of orange chairs, one behind the other, facing forward. This is where the prisoners sit until their case is heard and then they are either released or taken back into custody. In the courtroom itself are more rows of orange chairs for the friends and relatives of the accused, the curious, and the accused persons who are at liberty until their cases are decided. The courtroom usually holds about fifty people daily as the docket of as many as a hundred charges are patiently worked through.

This day, it was packed. Men and women filed in silently, quickly filling the chairs and lining the walls two or three deep. As they did so, police officers in plain clothes photographed the gathering from every angle. The front rows were filled quickly with journalists and Nerland's family and friends. From the Native people, there was a silence that was eerie and effective.

Judge Tom Ferris entered the courtroom and everyone stood until he was seated and the proceedings opened. The first order of business was the usual ban on publication. David LaChance would have to wait until the transcripts were ready if he was to know the details.

Every time Nerland said a word to police officers, it was noted. It was not policy, but Mesluck ordered that everything Nerland said outside of court, whether in cells or in the police van, be noted. It proved enlightening when his private comments later became public. Thus it was that Nerland brought himself to the attention of several uniformed officers who otherwise would have had little to do with him.

While waiting for his hearing to begin, Nerland was held in the cells behind the courtroom. Here, he suddenly decided to go on a kind of hunger strike, refusing to eat what he called "Gook food." The meals provided for police prisoners were prepared by Greeniss Restaurant, a well-known downtown Prince Albert café and store owned by a Chinese-Canadian family. "I won't eat that Chink food, I'll starve first. I won't eat anything unless it's prepared by a white man," Nerland snarled.

Nerland was brought handcuffed into the dock. He was cleanly shaven and neatly dressed. He seemed subdued and formal, but not nervous. He sat upright, looking straight ahead; only his face showed the contempt he held for the whole process — the contempt he had so vividly shown in his jail cell.

Nerland was heavily guarded, mostly for his own safety. There could have been a violent backlash from the First Nations; there were those who advocated it. Nerland feared the Indian people might kill him. But that is not how the Natives would deal with Leo LaChance's death. Once again trust was put in the treaty promises. Once again, the justice system had in its hands the faith of the First Nations. Their silence was their statement.

Once the bail hearing got underway, the Crown called its first witness, a Canada immigration officer, Christopher Allan Sowden of Calgary, who had interviewed Carney Milton Nerland in November 1985 at Calgary International Airport when Nerland had used the disguise of Kurt Meyer, American citizen, when he applied to "visit" Canada. He produced a Louisiana identity card, carried by citizens of that state, and a social security card, to "prove" his false identity. Kurt Meyer was also the pseudonym used by Nerland when he became the Saskatchewan leader of the Church of Jesus Christ Christian Aryan Nations in September 1990. The name was a jeer at the people of Saskatchewan who mourned twenty Canadian soldiers of the Regina Rifles Regiment, executed by the real Meyer in France in 1944.

Nerland, posing as Kurt Meyer, told the Calgary immigration officer he planned to visit friends in Red Deer and Edmonton. But when pressed to identify these friends, Nerland had been evasive and changed his story. He planned to visit friends in Vancouver, Nanaimo, Victoria, and Regina, he said, pulling out business cards from these people as proof of his intentions. Nerland told the immigration officer that he was a part-time baker. Then he said he actually worked at flea markets. His annual income, Nerland estimated, was three thousand dollars per year, yet he had a five hundred dollar return airline ticket, paid for in cash, and five hundred dollars spending money. From his luggage, Nerland produced business cards from various American suppliers of guns and Nazi paraphernalia, with notations of those who could supply hand grenades and automatic weapons. He carried photographs of himself in Nazi uniform and in combat training at Hayden Lake, Idaho, home of the Aryan Nations church. One of the photographs showed a uniformed Nerland using a rifle to bash in the head of a mannequin, an exercise that was part of his Nazi training. But there were more incriminating items in his suitcase. He also had audio tapes of Adolf Hitler and more Aryan Nations' tapes on interrogation techniques for extracting information. Nerland's own Nazi party membership card was there, along with Nazi paraphernalia that he said he intended to trade with his friends.

Yet, in the face of all this, Nerland denied any Aryan Nations or Nazi connections for himself. He told Sowden he was a member of an historical reenactment society. He had had nothing to say when he was asked about the photograph of his combat training.

In the courtroom, Sowden identified Carney Nerland as the Kurt Meyer of the Calgary interview. The immigration officer stated he had known "Meyer" was actually Carney Nerland in 1985, based on information about criminals and suspected dissidents shared by police and immigration officials. As a result, he had detained Nerland and then sent him back to the United States the following day. Nerland was ineligible for admission into Canada under Section 19-1h of the Immigration Act, which then stated: "he was not a genuine immigrant or visitor. . . ." The day after Sowden's interview with him, Nerland flew to Texas on Continental Airlines.

The Crown's next witness was Detective Sergeant Peter Mesluk. Mesluk began his story with the 911 call received at 6:34 P.M., 28 January, from Kim Koroll. Mesluk then talked about the arrival of the ambulance and said ambulance drivers had noted the smell of Lysol on LaChance's breath.

Mesluk continued his testimony: "It was a gunshot wound. It had passed through the left side of his chest and the bullet was . . . you could feel it on the skin on his right side. It hadn't left the body. It was just under the ribs." He described the police actions the night of the shooting: how Arnold Katz had let them into the building and oily footprints led them to the basement. There they found a door leading from Katz's basement, next door to a minirange scattered with spent shells and lead under the gun shop. Owners Darwin Bear and Nerland had been interviewed that same night and had accompanied police to the shop in the early hours of the following morning. At the time, Nerland had denied any knowledge of the incident but police said they would search the premises anyway. He finally gave a statement to police, describing two strangers who fired a gun when his back was turned. He added that they threatened him and then left. Nerland had told Mesluk in his statement that he was afraid when the strangers were in the shop because "there were guns all around." It was a gun shop after all.

Mesluk testified that Nerland had also said that he did not get a lot of business from Natives. Yet that contrasted directly with what Brownbridge had told the police officer, that Nerland had many Native customers and depended on their business.

Mesluk continued that the hole in the shop door indicated that the shot had travelled from the inside to the outside of the door. The door had been covered with a flag and he did not believe a person could see outside from inside the shop.

Mesluk described finding drinking glasses with traces of alcohol and cola, two fresh bullet holes in the floor, interviews with Nerland's father, McKnight, Yungwirth, and Brownbridge. He told of the trip by Nerland and the two others to Canadian Tire and he mentioned Nerland's telephone call in which he said he was going to Alberta to buy a van.

The Crime Stoppers calls warning police that Nerland was about to run were made 30 January. One of the callers indicated that neighbours in the Coronation, Alberta, area where Nerland had gone, might sympathize with his white supremacist views and therefore help him to flee. However, that information was not relayed to city police until 31 January. By then Nerland had been arrested. Now, Mesluk could only fervently hope that the information supplied by these calls would help keep Nerland in jail until the courts had dealt with him.

Just before the bail hearing Mesluk said police learned that

Nerland and his family had been given notice to vacate their rental unit and that Nerland's wife had tickets, valued at $3,100, for herself and their daughter, to fly to Chile on 4 March. Nerland had indicated he earned nine hundred dollars per month at the time. The police had asked how he had paid for the tickets. Friends provided the money, they were told. What kind of friends give that kind of money for a trip for someone else's wife, they wondered.

Mesluk's testimony connected Nerland to a rally of Aryan Nations and Ku Klux Klan members held in Provost, Alberta, in 1990 and to Terry Long, head of the Aryan Nations in Canada, then living in Caroline, Alberta.

But defense lawyer Earl Kalenith effectively reduced the strength of that testimony. "There is nothing from your investigations to indicate that the cause of death was in any way related to political beliefs. Is that correct?"

"That's right."

"In any way related to race?"

"That's right."

"Related to anything other than an accident?"

"As it stands now, yes, that's correct," Mesluk had to admit.

The prosecutor, John Field, impressed upon the court that the Crown had a strong case for manslaughter. "It is interesting to note that the accused's first reaction to the shooting is not that there was someone hurt, but that his business would suffer." He must have known he had probably hit someone, but he refused to let a passerby who was trying to help the victim telephone for help. The prosecutor continued his argument. Nerland was not likely to appear in court for trial if he were released. He had gone to extraordinary lengths to lie to the authorities, not only about the shooting but also during his abortive attempt to enter Canada under a false name in 1985. He was a member of a group that could assist his flight from justice. Field wanted Nerland held in jail until his trial.

In his bid to have Nerland released on bail, Kalenith pointed out that the Crown's own case suggested an accidental death and noted

Nerland had family support in Prince Albert. His mother, two brothers, and a sister were prepared to help him. Although Nerland might well choose not to live with relatives, the option was there. Nerland's gun shop business had been closed by police the night of the shooting, but Nerland had been a labourer before and could be again. A friend, Roy McKnight, was prepared to post the one thousand dollar bail, the amount suggested by the bail officer. Nerland's behaviour after the shooting and the flight to Alberta did not show intent to flee the country, Kalenith argued, because Nerland had told the police where he was going. And carrying two thousand dollars to buy a van from a neighbour of his father's was not an irregular thing to do. Nerland had no criminal record, other than some convictions as a juvenile, which could no longer be held against him. He had cooperated with police, and did not run after the shooting.

Judge Ferris postponed his decision on Nerland's release. When he did rule, three days later, what he had to say must have made Nerland suddenly see the wisdom of pleading guilty to manslaughter while he still could — to avoid a life sentence for murder.

Although this was a bail hearing to determine if Nerland could be freed until his forthcoming trial, Judge Ferris took time to comment on the evidence he had heard. He said Nerland's conduct after the shooting gave the court real cause for concern. The accused waited five hours before he went to police and then he told them he knew nothing about the shooting. The first story he told the detectives had two strangers enter his store as he was closing up for the evening and one had fired a weapon when Nerland's back was turned. The two men then threatened Nerland to keep his mouth shut and left. "If this statement were true and Nerland was worried about the two men in his shop, why did he not let Koroll, the passerby who wanted to help LaChance, use the telephone? Why had he not seized on the excuse the Good Samaritan provided and run out into the street to help the injured man? He must have known the fallen man had been shot," the judge remarked. Nerland had also indicated in his initial statement to police that the stranger could have picked up some bullets from the counter. But if the stranger had picked up ammunition, Ferris asked, "What was Nerland's excuse, as an experienced gun dealer, for leaving ammunition on the counter?"

Judge Ferris was also critical of the police on this point because he thought they should have asked Nerland why he did not know that a man must have been shot, especially when Koroll came in to call for help.

The judge suggested Carney Nerland might be committed to trial for a more serious charge than manslaughter — second degree murder. That was what people in Prince Albert wanted to hear. But much more was necessary to lay a more serious charge than people merely wanting Nerland to stand trial for murder.

Ferris explained what legal requirements would need to be met to raise a manslaughter charge to murder. A murder charge must prove beyond doubt that Nerland had intended to kill LaChance. It is one thing to know. It is another matter altogether to prove, he indicated. There would have to be hard evidence and that is what the public did not seem to understand.

At a bail hearing, Judge Ferris could not commit Nerland for the more serious charge. But he thought Nerland might be committed to trial for second degree murder at a preliminary hearing of the evidence, if the presiding judge were convinced that Nerland knew the gun was loaded, and fired it simply to amuse himself and the others by running Leo LaChance out of the store, or deliberately shot so close to the victim that he took the risk of injuring or killing him.

In their statements, Yungwirth and Brownbridge said an elderly, inebriated Native man entered the shop wanting to sell a .303 rifle, not furs as Leo had told police. Yungwirth heard a shot, followed by another shot as the victim walked out the doorway. Judge Ferris wondered why Yungwirth would take his eyes off Nerland, let alone why Yungwirth did not do something, or at least say something, about the first shot. Ferris also objected to Brownbridge's callous remark, "You silly bugger, you could have hit my car," when a man had been in the line of fire. No one went to LaChance's aid and no one offered a reason why not. Yet afterwards, in the car, the three men talked about whether the fallen man had slipped on the ice or been shot. Yungwirth later admitted to police he knew in his heart Leo LaChance had been hit. Ferris concluded, from these statements, that the men deliberately did not find out if the bullet from Nerland's gun had hit someone. Ferris wondered why Koroll would want to call 911 for someone who had merely passed out. It was unlikely and added to the doubt in Ferris's mind about Yungwirth and Brownbridge's honesty in saying they just did not know LaChance had been hit.

Ferris considered the three men, Nerland, Yungwirth, and Brownbridge, may very well have agreed on their statements before going to police but there was no real evidence they had done so. He wondered aloud if Brownbridge and Yungwirth had talked to Nerland while he was in Alberta and told him the details of their statements to police. If Nerland thought Sergeant Mesluk no longer believed him, he would have had more reason to run away at that point.

Ferris said he did not think the truth about the Alberta trip had come out yet. Nerland had gone to an area where there were others with white supremacist views and the judge suspected Nerland might still seek their help to leave Canada. The judge was also concerned that Bob Nerland had not told police he was living in Alberta. Had Carney really gone to buy a van from his father's neighbour in Alberta or had he gone to Coronation where white supremacists were believed to live, with two thousand dollars cash in his pocket, in order to escape?

The judge noted that the night of the shooting, Nerland had told Yungwirth and Brownbridge that his past would be used against him. And this was exactly what was happening. He had friends among white supremacists in Alberta, he had attended a rally in Provost, Alberta, in September 1990, and he had worked with David Duke in Louisiana in 1985. He lied to immigration officials about who he was. He carried photographs of himself in Nazi uniform undergoing military-style training at the Aryan Nations headquarters at Hayden Lake, Idaho. To Judge Ferris, that indicated a very strong desire to live out a fantasy.

Ferris wondered how a business such as Nerland and Bear's could sustain a two thousand dollar cash withdrawal on 29 January. Did Bear know Nerland had taken the cash to buy a van? When was this trip planned? If Nerland earned nine hundred dollars per month from the business, as he had told the bail officer, how had he just produced $3,100 for airline tickets for his wife and daughter's planned trip to Chile the following month? It certainly looked as though someone else was doing the financing, Ferris said.

Nerland's willingness to lie and blame others, his planning and deviousness, all weighed against him. The judge thought there might well be people in the Coronation area willing to help him flee. Daily reporting to a bail officer was not enough, Judge Ferris concluded. A person could go a long way overnight and the American border was within easy reach. Nerland would likely run if given a chance. Therefore, he would not have that chance.

Judge Ferris ruled that Carney Nerland must be held in custody in the remand centre at the Prince Albert Correctional Centre until the case against him was concluded.

On his way to back to jail, Nerland had the last word. "If I am convicted for shooting that Indian, you'll have to pin a medal on me. I've done you all a favour," he told the police.

CHAPTER FIFTEEN

Burning Crosses and Burning Questions

Nerland lied to the police in his statement made the night Leo LaChance was shot. But Gar Brownbridge's and Russ Yungwirth's accounts provided the basis for the charge that was laid. The problem was that the public could not believe that the shooting of an Indian by a white supremacist would only add up to manslaughter. It was cold-blooded murder, pure and simple, the people insisted.

The day after the shooting, Russ Yungwirth had engaged Prince Albert lawyer Martel Popescul, and Gar Brownbridge had hired one of Popescul's partners, Trent Forsyth. Both are considered to be among the city's best attorneys and both have extensive experience as Crown prosecutors and defense lawyers. They promptly advised the two men to tell their story to the police. They were interviewed by the police one hour after Nerland left town for Alberta and fourteen hours after Leo LaChance died of gunshot wounds. Sergeant Mesluk questioned Yungwirth while Sergeant Novotny talked to Brownbridge. The stories were nearly identical.

John Field, Peter Hryhorchuk, and Joe Kulyk were the Crown prosecutors who decided whether the charge would be murder or manslaughter. Technically they could have told police to lay a charge of first degree murder and then hope Nerland would at least be found guilty of the lesser charge of manslaughter. Few would have blamed them for doing so, and they knew the public was not going to be happy with a charge of manslaughter. But, at that point, two days after the shooting, they did not have proof beyond a reasonable doubt that Nerland had deliberately set out to murder LaChance. They felt the only ethical and correct thing to do was to lay a charge of manslaughter.

The Crown's theory of an accidental shooting was based on the beliefs that LaChance was outside the shop when he was shot, that his going into the shop was unplanned, and that there were no arguments or racial slurs while he was there. Most important, Nerland appeared "surprised" by the shot, even though he still had the rifle in his hands, pointed at the door.

Although the police and prosecutors were aware Nerland was a white supremacist and had taken part in the Aryan Fest at Provost, Alberta, they could not prove his racism had anything to do with the shooting of a Cree man. But this may have been the result of flaws in the investigation. First, the prosecutors had not ordered the police to look for proof or to examine in detail Nerland's racist leanings and the police saw no reason to do so. Second, the sophisticated capabilities of the RCMP forensic lab in Regina had not been used to full advantage to confirm that LaChance was outside the store when he was shot. Third, some believed the Crown should have laid murder, rather than manslaughter charges against Nerland, because once the charge of manslaughter was laid, no amount of evidence pointing to a murder could raise the charge to murder. With a manslaughter charge, Nerland could at maximum only be convicted of manslaughter.

In his decision at the bail hearing in February, Judge Ferris made it clear he thought the charge against Nerland might still be raised from manslaughter to murder at a preliminary hearing. But for a judge to decide at a preliminary hearing that manslaughter was an inappropriate charge, Ferris said, the trial would have to show intent to kill. What Leo LaChance told the police would have to be entered as evidence, and he had clearly said that the shooting was an accident and that only one shot was fired. But, Ferris pointed out, questions about LaChance's statement would be asked. "Did the victim get it right given his state of inebriation? Was there really only one shot fired? Was it an accident because Nerland didn't know the gun was loaded?" Ferris felt a mishap was very unlikely because Yungwirth and Brownbridge had spoken of more than one shot. The police had found two fresh bullet holes through the floor and a third in the door, which confirmed what Gar Brownbridge had said about hearing three shots. Judge Ferris said firing the weapon three times made an accident much more unlikely. "Nerland, as a gun shop owner, shouldn't have made a first mistake and if he had, he would have been expected to put the gun down after the first shot was fired. Ferris found the mishap theory even more unlikely because the witnesses had said Nerland had "raised the gun to his shoulder and 'accidentally' fired again," the judge noted.

Judge Ferris called this his "run-'em-out-the-door theory" and said it explained why Yungwirth and Brownbridge behaved as they did. "Why would Yungwirth say nothing after the first shots were fired? Why would Brownbridge say such a sickly macho thing as 'You silly bugger, you could have hit my car,' " Ferris asked. "Why didn't they look to see if LaChance was injured? Why did they refuse Koroll the use of the telephone when he came running in for help? How could an experienced gun handler accidentally fire three shots in two different directions? LaChance was not threatening Nerland."

It was an ugly theory and suggested "a sick outlook" as Ferris said, but it also was what most people suspected was the truth. It was the crux of the whole case. It was now known across Canada that Nerland was a white supremacist. People believed he had shot LaChance because Leo was an Indian and Nerland had no use for Indians. He was as careless of LaChance's life as a driver who hates cats and makes no attempt to avoid hitting one on the road. The fact that proving those theories about the shooting tragedy depended on the testimony of Nerland's friends was very frustrating for the court. Yungwirth and Brownbridge were Crown witnesses and the prosecutors could hardly cross-examine their own witnesses if the case came to trial.

But there was another wild card in the never ending debate over Carney Nerland. The white supremacist was also believed to be a paid police informer. This incredible factor was uncovered during the inquiry. Sergeant Mesluk told commissioners that police and prosecutors had been told the name of an RCMP informer when Corporal Lawrence met with them several days after the shooting. The RCMP were determined to keep the name of the informant a secret and the commission was equally determined that all the facts in the case must be laid before the public. The struggle went all the way to the Supreme Court of Canada before the right of police to keep informants' identity secret was upheld and the commission was forced to avoid any evidence that might tend to identify the informant in this case.

Nevertheless, the informant was publicly identified by the LaChance family and Chief A. J. Felix of the Prince Albert Tribal Council. *Globe and Mail* reporter Dave Roberts and CBC radio reporters released the same information, based on assurances from their independent sources. Testimony by Corporal Lawrence tended to support these beliefs when he told commissioners Nerland had telephoned him from jail. The call confirmed for Nerland that Lawrence could do nothing for him after he had been charged in the shooting death of Leo LaChance. Nerland was on his own. If Nerland was not an RCMP informant, why would he call Lawrence and what would he expect a police force not involved in the investigation to do about his situation?

The conclusion David LaChance reached was the same one the public reached, rightly or wrongly, that the police and prosecutors had gone easy on Nerland because he was an informant. David did not blame them, though. He figured it was their job to cover for an informant.

Brownbridge and Yungwirth said they knew little or nothing about Nerland's alleged white supremacist leanings. They said he had a Chilean wife, a Jewish landlord, and a Treaty Indian partner. He was friendly toward Natives and depended on their business. They said that Nerland was fearful that the police would "blow up the Native thing." They themselves had no such racist leanings and Nerland would clear them of any such involvement when he testified the following year. Nerland was "mischievous," an "asshole"; it was all a joke or an accident. There were many details they just could not recall from what was a very traumatic evening. Perhaps some people could understand how some things could be overlooked in an unexpected event of that magnitude, but David and Albert LaChance did not believe them. In their eyes, the two men were liars.

But the king of forgetfulness was Nerland himself. He did not even remember seeing Leo LaChance. He did not recall shooting him. He forgot he had his car at the shop that night and he did not remember driving around for an hour or more with Roy McKnight between the time he had finished dinner with his family until minutes before he went to the police station. It spawned one Nerland joke (after Nerland lost more than one hundred pounds to alter his appearance): How do you know it's really Nerland you are talking to? He can't remember his name, but he recalls that Alexander, king of Macedonia, rode a white stallion with a pink nose named Bucephalus on 29 September 331 BC.

There were little things that added to the public's suspicions. Nerland, his father, and his friends Gar Brownbridge and Roy McKnight were all unable to pinpoint the time these events had occurred. All four told police "I don't wear a watch." Brownbridge, Yungwirth, and Nerland claimed that they discussed the Gulf War for more than two hours. Nerland then discussed it for another hour and a half with Roy McKnight. The shooting was not discussed. Yungwirth, Nerland, and Brownbridge took weapons — three? six? or maybe it was nine rifles, they could not remember — with them on their trip to Canadian Tire immediately after the shooting. The explanation was that Nerland had a license to carry firearms, but there was no explanation as to why, on that night, he would want these dangerous weapons with him. Half an hour later, he brought the guns back to the shop and put them in the car. But he would tell police he had even forgotten that he had driven his car to the store that day.

Then there was the question of the oft-mentioned bearded man.

Kim Koroll had told police he remembered seeing a bearded man in the shop when he ran in to call 911. Was there someone else at the shop?

There were too many conveniently forgotten details to allow anyone to believe the stories they were hearing from the accused and the witnesses. The frustration of not being able find out the truth was bitterly galling to the family and to the public.

⸺⸺   ⸺⸺

After his bail hearing was concluded on 8 February, Nerland was returned to his cell in the remand centre of the Prince Albert provincial jail, where he stayed until his trial two months later.

The remand wing is removed from the main jail population. There is a row of single cells, a common room, and a private exercise yard.

Most prisoners hate it and will even plead guilty to minor crimes rather than sit in their cells in the remand centre for days, weeks, or months waiting for a trial that might prove them innocent. They refer to it as "dead time." Because they are not yet sentenced, they are not paid, they cannot take part in any programming and their movements are restricted to the remand centre, with twice-daily visits to the main gymnasium.

Nerland had once bravely said he would not mind jail because he had so many friends who were guards there. But in reality, he hated it as much as anybody. Other prisoners kicked his cell door as they passed, or cursed or threatened him. Many did what they could to make his life miserable because he was a known racist and the bulk of inmates in the jail are Native. He had visitors and they brought him cigarettes and other comforts, but it was a long, stressful time for Carney Nerland. Sometimes he gave other prisoners cigarettes in an attempt to ease relationships. Sometimes he talked about his hero Hitler and the Third Reich, but mostly he remained very much alone and very much disliked. Some inmates even telephoned to tell reporters that the boastful Mr. Nerland was not feeling so brave now he was inside.

Then, in late February, Earl Kalenith approached John Field and requested a meeting. His client was considering pleading guilty, he said, but he wanted it to be worth his while. If the public refused to believe that the shooting of Leo LaChance was anything but murder, despite the legal explanations, then this next development — plea bargaining — would be truly infuriating.

The prosecutor and defense lawyer met several times to discuss what the outcome would be if Nerland were to plead guilty to manslaughter. There were advantages to both sides. The case would be settled without a lengthy and costly trial. Nerland would escape many months waiting in the remand centre and he would be able to begin the prison term he knew he could not avoid. Better to get on with it. The legal points were worked through in detail; both lawyers studied cases with similarities to the shooting of LaChance, in order to decide what sentence was appropriate. At the time, two to five years was the sentencing range for manslaughter involving accident. It has since been increased — to three to seven years.

On 12 April 1991, Carney Nerland pleaded guilty to manslaughter in Court of Queen's Bench. The presiding judge, Mr. Justice W. F. Gerein, made it abundantly clear to Nerland that he was disgusted with his white supremacist beliefs, but that he was not taking them into account because they had not been placed before the court as part of the case. However, Gerein pointed out, had Nerland's racist background been presented as an argument concerning his motive for the shooting, then the sentence could have been increased. As it was, the judge was bound by the prescribed sentencing range. He sentenced Nerland to four years, to be served in the Prince Albert Correctional Centre.

This did not sit well with the public; four years was considered not enough for killing a man. In a telephone survey conducted by the Prince Albert *Daily Herald*, only 2 out of 187 callers thought the sentence was adequate. The outrage increased when Mr. Justice Gerein recommended Nerland serve his time in a provincial jail, rather than in a federal penitentiary. Eugene Arcand, a leader in the Prince Albert aboriginal community, was angry. "They send our guys to penitentiary and he gets to go to kindergarten!" The commissioner of the Correctional Service of Canada did not agree with Gerein either. Nerland was sent to Stony Mountain penitentiary, just outside of Winnipeg.

As Carney Nerland was escorted out of the court house, he spotted Leo's brother David and his wife and promptly gave them the finger.

CHAPTER SIXTEEN

The Community

The community could not accept what had happened. A man who headed the Aryan Nations, a white supremacist organization, had shot an Indian to death and been sentenced to a mere four years in prison. The case had not come to trial. After a year, still virtually nothing was known except Nerland had shot Leo to death and he had pleaded guilty to manslaughter. It was believed Carney Nerland was still the leader of the Saskatchewan Branch of the Church of Jesus Christ Christian Aryan Nations. News stories reported that Manitoba neo-Nazis considered Nerland a hero and visited him at Stony Mountain Penitentiary outside Winnipeg.

In the opinion of white and First Nations citizens, this was clearly a racist murder with deep repercussions. Were there more Nazis around? Would there be more murders? Would Nerland have been charged with murder if his victim had been a white man? Why was there no trial? Was there a cover-up?

David LaChance, for one, was not willing to leave it alone. There had to be a full explanation. The chiefs of the Tribal Council, representing the twelve bands in the Prince Albert area and northern Saskatchewan, also considered the matter and decided to demand answers from the Justice Department. But before they could proceed, they needed David's permission to press for an inquiry. The Big River band is not part of the Prince Albert Tribal Council, and so David was invited to meet with the chiefs and discuss the family's feelings about the speedy conviction and the unanswered questions it left. David gave permission on behalf of his family. A delegation that included Chief A. J. Felix, but not David LaChance, was sent to meet with then Justice Minister Gary Lane, at the provincial legislature in Regina. At the same time, Prince Albert Mayor Gordon Kirkby petitioned Lane and federal Attorney General Kim Campbell. Neither was responsive to the request for an inquiry.

But neither the city nor the Tribal Council would drop the matter. National Grand Chief Ovide Mercredi visited the city and agreed a formal commission of inquiry should be established. Others also questioned the handling of the incident. In the legislature, Keith Goulet, a Cree representing the northeastern quarter of the province, and Prince Albert area MLAs Myron Kowalsky and Eldon Lautermilch, all New Democrats, were willing to pressure their party to take action.

Two Alberta men, Harvey Kane, who heads the Jewish Defence League in Calgary and Keith Rutherford, in Edmonton, a retired CBC reporter who lost an eye in an Aryan Nations-led attack some years before, approached the Prince Albert Tribal Council as well as David LaChance. They had information on Nerland's behaviour at Provost the September before LaChance was killed. Television tapes and newspaper articles showed Nerland in his Nazi uniform, armed with a shotgun, taunting an elderly man dressed in a Second World War Nazi death camp uniform. Rutherford and Kane also provided the Prince Albert Native community with disturbing literature and information on the Aryan Nations and Ku Klux Klan movements in western Canada. It reinforced the determination to know more about the Nerland case and the possible presence of white supremacists in Prince Albert.

Local organizations, such as the Prince Albert Indian Métis Friendship Centre and the Saskatchewan Aboriginal Women's Council prepared their strategies. The Federation of Saskatchewan Indian Nations, headed by Chief Roland Crowe, announced its support and determination to hear the truth.

An organization with no counterpart in white society, the Grandmothers, appeared in the city 19 April 1991 and marched in silence through the streets. This gathering of Indian grandmothers, all of whom live in Saskatchewan, is not organized and has no set membership or program. When they feel they are needed, they spontaneously gather and go together to the source of the trouble to try to solve the problem. Following the Grandmothers' lead were a hundred or more aboriginals in Prince Albert, from politicians to street people. What they thought and what they wanted was clear: that the truth be told about Carney Nerland and his insidious white supremacist views. The Grandmothers, wearing their traditional shawls, formed two lines behind one of their number who set the pace and the mood with a slow, quiet, steady beat on the sacred drum in her hand. Two young women led the way, carrying a banner between them that said, "In memory of Leo LaChance." In silence they gathered at the steps of the courthouse and in silence they marched through the city, circling in front of city hall, before continuing to the place where Leo LaChance had been shot.

The Prince Albert *Daily Herald* had covered the case from the beginning and, in fact, had published a story only five hours after LaChance died. The *Herald*'s consistent theme was that the public must know what had really happened and justice must not only be done, it must be seen to be done. Still Justice Minister Lane flatly refused to grant an inquiry.

David LaChance was torn. He had faith in the white man's justice system. He believed the RCMP would do everything possible to learn the truth. But the information he was getting and the calls he was receiving from people he trusted were making him wonder: was something being covered up? Were things really as the police and courts had said? He wanted to hear from the two witnesses to the shooting — to learn exactly what had happened to his brother in the gun shop the night he was shot, and he wanted Nerland brought back to Prince Albert, this time to face a murder charge. David could no longer believe the shooting was an accident. What he had learned in the previous months convinced him Nerland had shot Leo because Nerland was a racist and Leo was a Cree.

One year to the day after Leo LaChance was killed, sixty family members, friends, supporters, community elders, and leaders gathered in protest in front of the former Northern Pawn and Gun Shop in Prince Albert. Standing in the background was a woman holding a wire ring of squirrel and weasel pelts, a sad reminder of the circumstances of Leo LaChance's death. Six pelts worth maybe five dollars. If he had arrived an hour earlier, he would have sold the skins to Arnold Katz and been on his way.

The questions continued, yet the march from the gun shop to the Indian Métis Friendship Centre on 29 January 1992 was not angry or noisy. Members of the family, including Leo's daughter Candace, led the way, carrying a banner saying "In memory of Leo LaChance." The demonstration maintained the quiet, dignified determination the LaChance family had displayed throughout the ordeal. Quiet, dignified, but utterly determined to get answers to their questions.

This was a day of feasting and prayers for the spirit of Leo LaChance, a tradition that was performed one year after the death of a Cree. More than 125 people gathered at the Indian and Métis Friendship Centre to cleanse themselves with burning sweet grass and to carry out an age-old ritual of healing for the family and for the community. A circle of thirty-eight men — leaders, elders, family, and supporters — sat in the centre. Prayers were said and a pipe was passed around the circle. Normally the ceremony would be held on the home reserve, but the family had chosen to hold it in Prince Albert because it was there Leo had been happiest. The LaChance family men took trays of stew and bannock to serve their guests.

But the determination of the aboriginal community to know what happened and to prevent another killing was not stilled that night. Chief Felix spoke about the need for healing and the request for prayers for the family and the people, yet he made it clear that the Tribal Council would persist until an inquiry was announced.

Lawrence Joseph, city alderman, Department of Indian Affairs official, and a contemporary of Leo's from the Big River Reserve, spoke directly to the issue. "All of Prince Albert is asking for some answers. We have no tolerance for loss of life, whether it is an accident or an outright crime. Prince Albert can't tolerate a loss of life, no matter how insignificant it might be. All races live here together, regardless of social standing. This [ceremony] is our way of saying: 'Let's give peace a chance. Let's heal together. No more tragedies!'"

Leo's death had already made a difference — the two races were finding common ground. Gathered for the ceremony were whites and Natives of every rank. As the group danced the slow measured steps of the round dance, the songs of a hurt people reached across Canada. The ceremony and the needs of the aboriginal people of Prince Albert were broadcast to the nation on CBC's "Sunday Morning."

Leo's sister, Roseanne Moses, and his niece, Sandra LaChance, agreed to interviews with the CBC and the Prince Albert *Daily Herald* that night. The two women were insistent on an inquiry. Roseanne said she was not content with the answers she had been given. "Why did that guy only get four years?" The explanation that sentences are based on precedent, that similar sentences are given out in similar cases did not satisfy her. She insisted this case was unique because Carney Nerland was involved with the Aryan Nations, a white supremacist group. "I believe he killed my brother on purpose and I think he should be charged [with murder]," she told reporters. She was the first to bring to light a contradiction she felt the two witnesses had perpetuated. Gar Brownbridge and Russell Yungwirth had told the police Leo LaChance had attempted to sell him a .303 rifle that night. "He never owned a .303 in his life," Roseanne insisted.

Sandra LaChance told the reporters, "They [the justice system] failed us. They failed my uncle by not looking at the facts. [The case] was dealt with very fast." Roseanne agreed. "If an Indian kills a white, it takes two or three years [to come to trial]. I guess my brother doesn't mean very much to anybody because this was a speedy trial. They didn't look at the facts around the case . . . they still haven't solved who killed our cousin."

Jean LaChance, twenty-nine, mother of five children, was found murdered 15 September 1991, in a farmer's field south of the Victoria Hospital in Prince Albert. Her murder was remarkably like the stabbing death of Leo's sister Virginia LaChance, at Taber, Alberta, some twenty-four years earlier. "It seems to me they are trying to cover up something [about Leo's death] that would come out in an inquiry," Roseanne said."I don't believe the police did their best at it. The Prince Albert Police Department knew a lot about Nerland. The system has let the family and the community down. It has raised tensions in this city. People are scared to talk. They are keeping quiet because they have been threatened not to talk. They don't have faith in the law because of this case. We want the truth! Who do we go to, who will protect us if not the legal system?"

The two women considered the recent tragic family history: Leo, shot to death in Prince Albert, Jean stabbed to death in Prince Albert, and Uncle Sam, who mysteriously disappeared from Prince Albert some years before.

"Why this family? Why here all the time? They all lived here at one time. I think something is going on that nobody knows about," Roseanne said.

Sandra expressed the hope that an inquiry would make people think twice before they did violence to Natives again. "It will change the way people look at Natives if the criminal justice system looks at this case and says 'Maybe there is a race relations problem in P.A.,' and then do something about it. Maybe they would stop letting people kill each other. [An inquiry] would put my faith back in the criminal justice system."

Some Natives shared the fears of the two women. A few did not. An observer of the march that morning said, "I look at [the killing] and say there are a lot of bigots around. Nerland was one of them . . . who wanted to be an idiot bigot and shoot a man. I say, 'That's your problem, guy.'"

The existence of an active white supremacist group in Saskatchewan was certainly plausible. Saskatchewan had had a very large Ku

Klux Klan organization during the Depression years. The revival of white supremacy theories in poor economic times sixty years later was believable.

It was known that Nerland was eligible for day parole as early as December 1991 and for full parole in August 1992. Indeed, he would be released under mandatory supervision in December 1993, after two-and-a-half years of his four-year sentence.

By 29 January 1992, Lane had resigned his justice portfolio and seat in the provincial legislature to become a judge at the Saskatchewan Court of Appeal. Bob Mitchell took over as minister and, on 10 February 1992, he announced an inquiry would be held into the death of Leo LaChance.

Canadian Press reporter Chris Wattie discovered that a review not a full-scale inquiry had been Mitchell's initial intent; however, he was soon to change his mind as the extent of the problems was revealed.

The province had chosen E. N. (Ted) Hughes, former justice of the Court of Queen's Bench in Saskatchewan and experienced head of inquiries into judicial matters. Hughes had left the bench in Saskatchewan to join the British Columbia Department of Justice in 1980 and had moved to the attorney general of British Columbia's staff in 1983. It was Hughes who sat on the bench during the property trial of former Saskatchewan cabinet minister Colin Thatcher and his estranged wife JoAnne. Since retiring from the Court of Queen's Bench, Hughes had been living in British Columbia where he held a number of influential positions in the justice system, including involvement in other judicial inquiries.

The City of Prince Albert chose the dean of the University of Saskatchewan College of Law, Peter MacKinnon. MacKinnon is a recognized expert on evidentiary matters but he has not defended a case in the courtroom. He is respected for a sharp mind and noted for his good manners and a friendly demeanour.

The Prince Albert Tribal Council and the LaChance family chose Delia Opekokew, a Toronto lawyer with extensive experience with legal issues affecting Native interests. Opekokew, a Cree woman, was raised in northern Saskatchewan, on the Canoe Lake Reserve. She had served for a time as legal counsel to the Federation of Saskatchewan Indian Nations.

The three commissioners met in MacKinnon's law faculty office in Saskatoon and within hours decided to tell Mitchell that nothing but a full-scale inquiry would be acceptable.

An editorial in the Prince Albert *Daily Herald* warned: "Nerland's sentence cannot be extended, no matter how unfair that might seem to some. The charges against Nerland also cannot be changed now. He cannot be tried, at this point, for the murder of LaChance.

"What the inquiry can do is see to it all of the information about the case is provided by the witnesses and police. Lawyers representing the LaChance family, the Prince Albert Tribal Council and the police and courts are able to examine the witnesses in detail."

But what about Nerland? What if he did not want to appear before a commission of inquiry? Could he avoid it? Apparently he could. He would just say No.

CHAPTER SEVENTEEN

The Inquiry

26 May 1992

The inquiry was more than a formal "whodunnit," a reexamination of the Carney Milton Nerland manslaughter case. Whether the public accepted it or not, Nerland could not be tried for the murder of Leo LaChance because he had already been convicted of manslaughter and the sentence could not be changed. This time it was not Nerland but the justice system itself on trial.

The mandate of the commission of inquiry spelled that out quite clearly. The commissioners were to examine how the City of Prince Albert Police Department and the prosecutors did their jobs. Did they investigate fully? Did the prosecutor lay the right charge? Did the prosecutor act properly in disposing of the charge of manslaughter? Should Nerland ever have been given a license to have and sell guns? Did the police act in good faith? Were they influenced by the RCMP's need to protect an informer? The commissioners were also to investigate whether and to what extent racist activity was connected to the shooting; whether that affected the police investigation or the legal process and whether the commissioners felt a further inquiry or more investigation into organized racist activity not connected with the death of Leo LaChance would be necessary.

The chair of the three-member commission, E. N. (Ted) Hughes, Q.C., is a tall man with wavy white hair and a grandfatherly appearance that in no way detracts from his imposing presence.

Each witness was to be examined first by commission counsel Morris Bodnar and then questioned by each of the lawyers representing the police, the prosecutors, the LaChance family, the RCMP, and the courts.

Bodnar, the commission lawyer, acting as a prosecutor, is a well-known defense lawyer from Saskatoon, now a member of parliament from that city. He is a tall, heavy set, balding man whose trademarks are his confidence, humour, and adaptability to every twist and turn of the inquiry and his ability to draw a mass of information from witnesses. His position at the inquiry was not without irony. As a well-known defense attorney, he had faced each of the province's seven top Crown prosecutors as an adversary. At the inquiry, he became the prosecutor that put each of the seven on the witness stand and questioned his participation in the administration of the LaChance case.

On 26 May, he set out his intentions for the inquiry proceedings: "It is hoped that the sequence of events will show and the evidence will show before the commission, that on January 28, 1991, at approximately 3 P.M. Carney Nerland's father had been to visit him at the shop. At about 4 P.M., his former partner, Darwin Bear, also visited him. At 5 P.M., a further friend, Roy McKnight, had visited him and left. At 5:15, two witnesses, being individuals by the name of Brownbridge and Yungwirth, arrived at his store, and I mention this more particularly because they, to our understanding, were witnesses to the shooting that occurred. At 5:30, the landlord of the premises in question, who operated the business next door, locked up his half of the building and left the vicinity. Approximately 6:30 P.M., Leo LaChance arrived and the shooting took place. At 6:35, an individual by the name of Kim Koroll spotted LaChance on the street and came to his help and attempted to phone help at that particular time. At 6:42, the ambulance arrived. At 6:45, Maurice Morin, a passerby, had spoken a few words to Leo LaChance. [Actually, this occurred a few moments before the ambulance arrived.] At 6:45 as well, the police arrived. At 7 P.M., Carney Nerland went to his sister's for supper. At 7:55, Constable Troy Cooper spoke to the deceased in a hospital in Prince Albert and obtained statements from the deceased. At 9:40, Sgt. Terry Cline and Sgt. Ed Koolick of the Saskatoon Police Department spoke, as well, to Leo LaChance while he was in hospital at the Royal University Hospital in Saskatoon and obtained further statements from Leo LaChance. It is our intention to lead those statements before this commission.

"January 29, at 12:55 A.M., which is just after midnight, Leo LaChance passed away. At 12:35 A.M., Carney Nerland was present in the police station at Prince Albert and gave a statement to the Prince Albert police, which we intend to show as false. At 3:15 A.M. [the inquiry report states 4 A.M.], Mr. Nerland and his partner Darwin Bear tried to get into the store to get some items, but the Prince Albert police turned them away. At 2 P.M. of that same day, two witnesses, Gar Brownbridge and Russ Yungwirth, were interviewed by the police after they voluntarily came forward. On January 30th, at 4:15 P.M., Carney Nerland was arrested in Alberta.

"That is a brief summary of the facts. From that point, the investigation was conducted by different members of the Prince Albert police. The information was taken to members of the Attorney General's Department in Prince Albert, a discussion was held and a charge of manslaughter was laid. Subsequent to this, Mr. Nerland entered a guilty plea and was sentenced by Mr. Justice Gerein to a term of four years on a joint submission by Defence and Crown. The matter of appropriateness of charge and sentence was reviewed to our understanding, by the Attorney General's office in Regina before final determination of this case." Bodnar indicated he would call witnesses in the order of their appearance in this chronology of events.

Before the first witness was called on 26 May, lawyer Marty Popescul, representing the RCMP, asked for an in-camera ruling on matters of evidence. From the beginning, Commissioner Ted Hughes had insisted that the inquiry be open in every way possible, yet secrecy was to play a dramatic role. Popescul wanted a ruling on the admissibility of certain evidence and because of the nature of that evidence, he wanted the commission to hear it in private. He wanted a ruling in place so the counsellors would know how to deal with certain evidence. Hughes made his stand clear: he would not hear any evidence in-camera and whatever it was Popescul felt was so delicate that it must be dealt with behind closed doors, would nevertheless be brought to the public at the earliest possible moment. The matter would be heard in a closed session at the end of the day.

For the time being, the commission proceeded with its first day of hearings. But the inquiry established to determine what exactly had happened the night Leo LaChance was shot was immediately faced with new mysteries that would remain mysteries — despite the commissioners determined efforts to solve them. Was LaChance leaving the shop at the moment he was shot? Was he actually closing the door from the outside at that moment?

The mysteries concerning how and where LaChance was shot took centre stage the moment the testimony of a police witness contradicted the police's own investigation.

Until LaChance's own words were repeated that day, the public understood that the shot rang out just as the door clicked shut when he left the store. The evidence of the bullet hole in the door and later witness testimony bore out this theory. But City Police Constable Troy Cooper, who had interviewed the wounded man at the hospital, told the commissioners Leo told him he 'was shot and left the store,' leaving the policeman with the impression LaChance was inside the store when he was shot. A Saskatoon police officer, Sergeant Terry Cline, got the same impression from LaChance when he interviewed the wounded man just prior to surgery in Saskatoon that night. Cline only learned the official version — that LaChance was shot outside the gun shop — after reading a newspaper. City police, searching the shop the night of the shooting, discovered a bullet hole through the door at chest height, 1.3 metres from the floor. Their theory on the sequence of events was confirmed by the two witnesses to the shooting, Yungwirth and Brownbridge, the following day. The new information provided by a seriously wounded man, gasping for each breath and in too much pain to worry about syntax, became the focus of much controversy.

The RCMP forensic expert on weapons, Staff Sergeant A. J. Somers, took the stand. He had been a Mountie for thirty years, twenty of them spent in the forensic laboratory attached to the Firearms Identification Section. For the past twelve years, he had headed the section and he had testified, as an expert witness, at dozens of trials in Saskatchewan and elsewhere.

The confusion that arose from his testimony had nothing to do with the forensic examinations he had performed for the LaChance investigation, but rather, because he was asked for his opinions on the case. He told the inquiry he had not seen the marks on the bullet he would have expected to find if it had gone through both a door and a human bone. The marks were consistent with a bullet hitting a bone, he said. He said it was possible that the bullet Nerland had shot went through a door and LaChance's arm; but he did not think it was probable based on his knowledge. If this were true, then it meant LaChance had been shot inside the store and then left, a complete contradiction of the witnesses' evidence and the city police findings.

Another question arose: why would Nerland shoot LaChance inside the shop and then shove him out the door if he was still alive? Was he smart enough to cover up all that? The testimony of 27 May ended with questions that would never be fully answered.

The commissioners were left with a lingering doubt about whether LaChance was inside or outside the shop when he was shot. But David LaChance was convinced Leo was shot while he was inside Nerland's place, and then, after he left, a second shot was fired through the door. Why? "Probably because Nerland wanted to shoot an Indian," David LaChance says. "They wanted to do whatever they wanted in that shop: drink, shoot. The police were in the shop several times every day it seemed and nothing happened. Nerland concluded he had nothing to worry about; he could do as he pleased." Policemen did frequent the shop. Could Nerland interpret their presence as approval of him and his attitudes, even to the point of "getting away with murder?" These were questions that would haunt the inquiry during its entire nine weeks of sitting. But on those first days, there was still the thorny disagreement on what facts could be revealed to the public.

The three commissioners and the eight lawyers representing the interested parties retreated into an in-camera session to discuss Popescul's request regarding the delicacy of some future testimony. The commissioners had said everything would be made public. That was what the First Nations expected. In Indian tradition, when it is agreed that a subject must be discussed, absolutely nothing can be held back. Hughes put it bluntly: the commission and counsellors had already held an in-camera session 26 May to discuss Popescul's request made on behalf of the RCMP. They were now going into a second in-camera session to conclude the arguments. It would not take long. The commissioners would then make a ruling. They were debating an interesting question: Could evidence that might reveal the name of a secret RCMP informant be kept out of the proceedings?

Peter MacKinnon delivered the commissioners' decision at 4 P.M. Friday, 28 May. Police informant privilege exists to protect the identity of informers and facilitate the gathering of information concerning criminal activities from them. But, so early in the inquiry, the commissioners could not foresee a need for such a ruling and therefore they refused to make one. At that point, no one really knew what kind of problems the decision was going to cause, but it certainly gave the spectators and reporters reason to pay attention.

Lawyer Gerry Allbright wanted the inquiry to decide where Leo LaChance had been when he was shot. His concern was for his clients, the members of the Prince Albert Police Association. Was it inside or outside the gun shop? Allbright knew there were two witnesses who had been in the store when the shooting happened. They could answer the question. Was it possible to hear those people next?

Allbright had already spoken to Commission Counsel about it. Bodnar set the priorities; he decided who spoke and when, and he was not inclined to change the lineup. The story was confusing enough. Bodnar felt if the eye witnesses were heard before the investigating officers, continuity would be lost. The officers had done a good part of their investigation without knowing there had been any witnesses to the shooting. He wanted the inquiry to hear testimony in the order the story had unfolded between 28-30 January 1991. Although Allbright had good reasons for wanting one thread followed to its conclusion, Bodnar had his own reasons for unbraiding the skein of threads in the order he planned. The commissioners ruled in Bodnar's favour.

Bodnar had planned to recall Corporal Bruce Parker, the city police identification officer who had brought the police photographs to the commission, to explain the remainder of the photographs. How could anyone know the impact his testimony was going to have?

However, before Parker could be recalled, Harold Pick, counsel for the Crown prosecutors, rose to address the commissioners: "With some trepidation before we all go out into that wonderful sunshine again, and enjoy the evening, I have one or two matters to discuss at this time, if I may be permitted to do so. I was directed unequivocally to place on the record the fact that Mr. Nerland is not represented by counsel at these proceedings although his name has come up repeatedly during the course of these proceedings, and it has been bandied about in the press, in what has been described to me as a most derogatory fashion. I don't read the press, maybe I'm lucky, but I'm simply placing on the record, and seeking any instructions or suggestions you may have regarding the fact that this man, who is one of the principal actors in this unpleasant and tragic drama is not represented by counsel at these proceedings. I have done that, and if you wish me to do so, I shall pass on to another topic that is more timely."

Bodnar reminded those present that Nerland had been invited to take standing at the inquiry and had refused both standing and legal representation. Pick continued, saying that Staff Sergeant A. J. Somers, the ballistics expert who had testified the previous day, was not bound by rules of evidence. He had therefore wandered into highly speculative areas (that the bullet did not bear the markings he would expect if it had passed through a door before striking LaChance). As a result, Pick said, Somers had forgotten to tell the inquiry of his other connection with the case, a connection Bodnar did not know about. There was a five-minute break while Pick explained this connection to Bodnar.

If Somers had another important link with the case, however, the inquiry was not going to hear about it. Instead, Pick asked the commissioners to bring a second ballistics expert into the proceedings, Shane Joseph Kirby, a former RCMP staff sergeant, retired for more than a decade from the position Somers then held in Regina. Pick identified Kirby as one of the foremost ballistics experts in Canada. Pick was granted an order that allowed Kirby to take the gun and projectile to perform further tests. A scheduled ten-day break in the proceedings would give Kirby enough time to examine the gun and the projectile from the bullet. His task was to try to settle the question: Was LaChance shot inside or outside Nerland's shop? The various groups then dispersed into the wonderful sunlight and what little was left of the evening.

On 29 May 1992, the lawyers studied stacks of photographs of the scene with a calm, experienced officer who explained the details if necessary. The place where LaChance had fallen after he was shot offered nothing. It was a much trampled section of city sidewalk, marked by a spot of saliva. There were no clues there. The lawyers found the photographs of the store, inside and out, much more informative. The Northern Pawn and Gun Shop faces the river, with two show windows, one on either side of the door. The door is recessed between the windows, about four feet back from from the city sidewalk, with a slightly upward sloping sidewalk of its own. At the doorway, the windows are only inches from the door frame. At the street, they are flared outwards to be several feet apart.

Identification Officer Bruce Parker had first visited the shop the night of the shooting. He had taken a few pictures then, more in the hours after midnight, and still more in the following days. Officer Parker had also seized a number of items as evidence, including the semiautomatic rifle used to shoot LaChance. When the gun was seized, the police had only Nerland's statement that one of two unwelcome men had possibly fired it in his store. The first items to indicate Nerland was lying were three drinking glasses, with no identifiable prints, that smelled of rye and cola. If Nerland had been trying to discourage and get rid of two strangers then it seemed unlikely they would have been drinking together.

But the major discovery was the hole in the door. In the photo it is obscured by the flag covering most of the door. In another photo, Detective Sergeant Novotny is holding a probe in the hole, which shows the trajectory of the bullet, past Nerland who is leaning on the counter, to a position behind the table at the back of the room. On Parker's diagram, this position is marked with a large X. Near it are two fresh bullet holes through the floor. At that point, the detectives did not know who had fired shots, how many, or from where. They knew only Nerland's story.

At the inquiry, the lawyers knew Nerland had fired two shots into the floor and one through the door from behind the counter. They wanted to know what evidence had been gathered in that regard. Did Parker ask about gunpowder burns on the flag covering the door? No. On LaChance's clothing? Yes. Did he seize the spent bullets from the floor? Yes. And the damaged section of door? Yes. Had he asked if the bullet that killed LaChance had also passed through the door? No.

Parker had also seized and sealed a gun case containing the weapon in question and had it hand-delivered to the forensic lab in Regina. There, Somers had been asked only if that gun had fired the bullet removed from Leo LaChance's chest. The case, with one mysterious compartment sealed and never opened by police, had been returned to Roy McKnight, the man who would have become Nerland's partner, if the shooting had not taken place and the shop had not been closed.

Sy Halyk, counsel for the courts involved, promptly asked the commissioners to enter an additional sixty or seventy photographs Parker had taken of the scene but had not prepared for the commission in the original submission. The commissioners agreed they needed to examine all of the photographs, not just those chosen by representatives of the police department. The lawyers also had questions for Parker.

Could LaChance have been shot inside the store, opened the

door by himself and left the store? Parker said it was possible. Could LaChance have fit in the space outside the door, sideways, so his left arm was in the position necessary to receive the bullet? The lawyers did not think so. This author has tried it. Opening the door from the inside, with the left hand, stepping through and pulling it shut behind, causes a person to turn so that the left side is at right angles to the door in the correct position to line up with the bullet hole.

City Solicitor Jean Maksymiuk, representing the police department, established that it was possible for someone inside the store to see through the glass at the bottom of the door, under the flag, even at night. If Nerland looked, it was possible he could have seen LaChance's lower legs and known he was still there when the shot was fired. But Parker testified he had not conducted a test to prove this theory.

Although this theory caused a murmur, the last questions Maksymiuk asked Parker were what stunned the listeners. "Now, in your twenty-one years at the Prince Albert Police Department, is it fair to say that you've gotten to know past and present members pretty well?"

"Yes, I would say so," Parker replied.

"Could you tell the commission whether you know of any attitudes of past or present members of the Police Department in regard to any sympathies with white supremacy or any racist organizations?" she asked.

"I find that question difficult to answer," Parker said. "My . . . personal knowledge is that there are sympathizers of that organization."

"Within the Police Department?" Maksymiuk asked.

"Yes. . . ."

"Was there anybody involved with this case, of that nature of sympathy, to your knowledge?"

"No, I don't believe there was," Parker said.

"[Have] such attitudes . . . come to your attention since this case has occurred, or prior to it?"

"I would say more so since this case has occurred. . . ."

"And in terms of the attitudes you're speaking of, could you describe what you are referring to?"

"At the present time I am not prepared to go into detail on that, at the risk of losing my employment," Parker answered.

"Are you referring to attitudes or involvements with organizations?"

"I would say attitudes, not involvement."

"Do you have any knowledge as to the existence of a white supremacist organization within the City of Prince Albert?"

"I don't have any personal knowledge of a particular existence of a . . . of an organization, no."

Bruce Parker always identifies himself simply as a Canadian. But what mattered to the audience was that he is an aboriginal Canadian and he said there were white supremacist sympathizers on the Prince Albert police force. Parker had good reason to make these remarks before the commission. He had seen something disturbing that, unknown to him then, was part of a covert police action. One of his fellow officers had a belt buckle with a white supremacist symbol. There were various other bits of Nazi and Ku Klux Klan paraphernalia among that officer's possessions kept in the locker room. It would be ten months before everyone knew about the secret operation; ten months of speculation and accusations against the police in Prince Albert.

Police morale was flagging. One officer angrily told a reporter, "I have served everyone in this community fairly for twenty-three years. If they are going to accuse me of racism after twenty-three years, they can have my badge right now and I'll quit!"

Cree Lawyer Gerald Morin, representing the LaChance family and the Tribal Council, did not allow himself to be swayed from his purpose by the startling announcement about white supremacists on the police force. He would get to that in time. His clients were concerned that members of the police force had not investigated this case as thoroughly as they should have. For example, Parker had called the killing a murder in his report to the RCMP forensic lab, yet the charge laid against Nerland on that same day was manslaughter. Why? Parker did not have personal knowledge of the eye witness reports that the Crown prosecutor used to arrive at a decision regarding the charge.

Parker had said that he had not found anything unusual in the investigation yet in one photo he had taken, the accused, Carney Nerland, had appeared. Was it not unusual for the chief suspect to be present at the investigation? Yes, Parker thought that was unusual, but Harold Pick, counsel for the Crown prosecutors, did not. He reminded the commission that Nerland was not the accused in the early hours of 29 January, when the photographs were taken. At that point, the detectives were still working on Nerland's tale of two strangers in his store.

Parker further testified that bullet holes in the floor, walls, and ceiling of the store were not examined closely although he had photographed them. He picked up only a few of the many bullet fragments in the basement. He would have had to dismantle the entire basement to get all the spent bullets, he told Morin. But Morin asked whether police were required to gather all evidence relating to firearms according to the section on firearms in the policy manual issued by the forensic lab. Parker said yes. Was all the evidence gathered in this case? No, Parker admitted.

Parker was asked why he had not removed the door or a section of it, to analyse it further. "Cost," Parker answered. His superiors told him there were concerns about the cost of replacement or damage to the door. A section of the door had been removed 31 January but it was not until the commission of inquiry considered the matter in May 1992 that removal of the entire door for analysis was finally considered affordable. Morin and Parker and city solicitor Jean Maksmiuk both believed that, if Carney Nerland had looked, he could have seen Leo LaChance through the glass under the flag on the door.

The guncase photographs interested Morin considerably. The gun case had been found behind the counter of the store, just behind the spot where Nerland had probably stood when the shots where fired. In addition to the semiautomatic rifle used in the shooting and an empty pistol case there was a small locked compartment which was never opened by police. Why not? There was no key, Morin was told. And again, budgetary restraints prohibited forcing it open because if it had been damaged, then it would have had to be repaired or replaced. Parker admitted it might have contained relevant evidence.

Harold Pick pointed out that Parker was not the investigating officer. His job was to take photographs and gather evidence. In the early morning hours of 29 January, Parker had no idea what Nerland had said in his statement to police just an hour before so he would not be aware of the possible significance of some evidence.

Morris Bodnar then returned to the question of alleged white supremacists, which he assumed were Aryan Nations sympathizers, on the city police force. Did those beliefs affect the investigation of this case? Parker had not noticed any effects. He did not believe racist views played any part in this inquiry. He thought that officers Demkiw, Novotny, and Mesluk had carried out their duties to the best of their abilities. Commissioner Delia Opekokew then asked Parker: Are the majority of people who come to the attention of the police in Prince Albert in fact Indian people? "Given our population base, I would say yes," Parker replied. The population of the city then was estimated at thirty percent Native.

Parker was then asked whether there was a telephone in the Northern Pawn and Gun Shop on the night of the shooting. Parker told the commission there was indeed a telephone; he had used it himself that night and yes, it worked just fine.

Parker was commended by the commissioners for his frankness and honesty. Speaking openly about his suspicions of white supremacist sympathies on the police force was courageous given the criticism his remarks were bound to raise. Parker left the stand, but the inquiry was just beginning its examination of the actions, real or imagined, of the Prince Albert City Police.

CHAPTER EIGHTEEN

Buried in the Silence

Most people are unfamiliar with police procedure and most police officers like it that way. But in this case, common misconceptions of police methods and protocol led to controversy and extra costs without satisfying anyone. There was confusion over several issues: who had investigated the case, the Mounties or the city police; why Nerland had not had a trial, and that in an inquiry, which is not a court case, opinions by the RCMP forensic experts, in particular, seemed to contradict what other police had already said were the facts in the case. It became imperative for the inquiry to spend the additional time and money to clear up the growing confusion.

Two police forces work in the Prince Albert area: the Prince Albert City Police and the RCMP. Because the city police force is local and the RCMP is federal, it is often thought that the Mounties have more authority in Prince Albert and that they will conduct investigations into major crimes in the city. This is simply not the case. If an RCMP officer were murdered in Prince Albert, the city police would investigate, not the Mounties.

The difference is a matter of territory. Anything within the city limits is the purvue of the city police. Anything within the detachment area, roughly fifty kilometres around the city, is the business of the RCMP. Thus a citizen might talk to the RCMP about a theft from his cottage, but would deal with the city police if the same crime were committed at his home.

Because Leo LaChance was shot in the city, the investigation should have been carried out entirely by the city police force. Yet the Mounties were a presence, and this helped muddy the waters.

Although Corporal Parker saw a local RCMP officer at the gun shop two days after the shooting and mentioned the fact at the inquiry, it was established that Jerry Tysowski had been there in his private capacity as a gunsmith, and not as a police officer.

The RCMP were quickly drawn into the investigation formally, through the forensic laboratory in Regina at F Division headquarters. All police forces within the division, RCMP or municipal, use this laboratory for forensic testing.

The RCMP were also involved once retired officer Shane Kirby was asked to perform additional firearms testing. Kirby had examined the gun shop door and the bullets Somers had then fired through it while carrying out forensic tests at the RCMP lab, and he performed a few tests of his own as well. The Department of Natural Resources had provided him with a deer that had been killed on the highway. At a local gun range, the frozen carcass was hung from an upright and the door was suspended four feet in front of it. Sergeant Novotny fired two rounds through the door, just above the lock, exactly where it was thought the fatal shot had passed through the door and through Leo LaChance's arm, before lodging in his chest. One bullet passed through the deer carcass. A second lodged on the far side of the deer's chest cavity. The velocity of the bullet as it left the muzzle was much higher than either Kirby or Somers had expected it to be and much higher than even the ammunitions manufacturer had said it would be. The bullet was quite capable of killing, even after penetrating a two-inch thick-wooden door. Clearly, Leo LaChance could have been shot outside the gun shop.

During Kirby's testimony, another contradiction arose from the findings of the two firearms experts. Somers had said that the bullet that killed LaChance did not have the markings he expected it to have if it had passed through a wooden door. He said the bullets used in the test with the deer carcass did have such striations. Kirby added to the confusion. He said first that the bullet striations in the deer carcass test were probably caused because the ammunition was forty to fifty years old. Then he added he had not seen any such markings on the bullets Somers had shot through the door (which were from the same box of bullets). "Just because I didn't see them doesn't mean they weren't there," he told Bodnar.

The problem seemed to stem from the fact that neither man often saw full-metal jacketed ammunition in their line of work. Most bullets have a soft lead tip that mushrooms on impact and causes widespread damage inside the victim. But the bullet used to kill LaChance was the type used by the military. Not many civilians use this type of bullet. The entire projectile is encased in brass and it retains its shape after striking the victim. This type of bullet is used by armies to disable rather than kill the enemy. LaChance died because the bullet bored a tunnel through his vital organs and the damage was irreparable.

The RCMP involvement that truly swept the inquiry off the tracks and left it derailed for months was something quite different — was Carney Nerland to be revealed as an RCMP informant? The commissioners were made aware of the the problem of the informant's identity on the first day of the hearings. However, the storm did not break for another month, during the third sitting of the inquiry. By prearrangement, the commission decided to ask a question asked that brought the informant issue to a head. Commission counsel Morris Bodnar asked Mesluk point blank: "What name was given to you as the name of the informant?" Popescul immediately stood up and registered an objection to the question. He then asked the commission for a ruling: Would the commission allow the name of the informant to be stated publicly?

There was a five-minute break before commissioner Peter MacKinnon posed another question to Sergeant Mesluk, warning him not to answer until counsel had had an opportunity to object to the question or not. MacKinnon asked: "Was the informant, whose identity was revealed to you by Corporal Lawrence, anyone who has an interest in the outcome of these proceedings, or anyone whose conduct is under review in these proceedings?" Popescul was prompt in his objection, suggesting the answer to the question might reveal the identity of the informant. Gerry Allbright, lawyer for the Police Association, of which Mesluk was a member, agreed with Popescul.

Now the problem was out in the open and the commission was prepared to deal with it. It was unquestionably a tough one for the commission, for they had promised a completely open hearing. Could they hold to this promise? Information provided by paid informants is used by all police forces and it is invaluable to them. But if the identities of the informants are revealed, surely they would no longer perform this role. Would the protection of informants take precedence over the right of the public to know the whole truth?

The commission broke for an in-camera session with the various lawyers. A few hours later, at 5 P.M., Commissioner Hughes announced their ruling. The right of the public to know the whole truth superseded the right of police to protect informants. Detective Mesluk was told to identify the informant.

Two questions were asked of Mesluk in-camera: what name was given to him, and was the informant someone who had an interest, or whose conduct was under review, in the proceedings of the inquiry? Gerry Morin and Gerry Allbright had supported the release of the informant's name at the hearing. But Marty Popescul had argued against releasing it. He would now take the tricky question to the Saskatchewan Court of Appeal.

Despite the uncertainty, the inquiry heard one more day of testimony on 29 June, and then adjourned for two months during the summer. Two days later, the Canadian Broadcasting Corporation and the Toronto *Globe and Mail* released stories identifying Carney Nerland as the RCMP informer.

On 6 August, the Saskatchewan Court of Appeal overturned the commission's ruling. Sergeant Mesluk would not be allowed to reveal the informant's name, despite the fact that most people in Saskatchewan and many in Canada knew that Carney Nerland was that man. According to the Court of Appeal, the informant privilege rule was beyond question.

Ted Hughes was not happy that the commission's argument was not considered by the Court of Appeal. On 24 August, the day the inquiry was to reconvene, he commented, "First, we recognize the importance and the reasoning behind the secrecy rule based on the public interest with respect to police informers' identity. We believe there are good and sound reasons for its existence that go to the preservation of the essential effectiveness of criminal law. It would be in the rarest of cases that it would be superseded. Secondly, this is one of those rarest cases, and it arises because the second public interest described by the commission in its June 25th ruling is, in the Commission's opinion, the dominant one. And that is because the heart and soul of the mandate of this commission is to determine whether, in this instance, the Justice system of this province worked fairly and with an extremely even hand. The fact that we are to consider and report on the integrity, objectiveness and good faith of the police investigation and the subsequent prosecutorial process, assessing as we do, whether organized racist activity affected that investigation or process is, we believe, decisive on the issue of the dominant public interest."

Hughes said the commission had already put the second question, whether the informant was someone who had an interest in the outcome of the inquiry or whose conduct is under review by the commission, to Sergeant Mesluk in the in-camera session held 25 June. Mesluk had answered "Yes." That had helped the commission to decide the dominant interest: having all the facts made public. It was extremely important to the work of the inquiry to have the name revealed, Hughes said. How else could it determine if the knowledge of the informant's identity had any effect on how the city police and the Crown prosecutors did their jobs? The identity of the person named as the informer had to be made public. The commission was taking the matter to the Supreme Court of Canada and the inquiry was put on hold until further notice.

The Supreme Court application was not the only legal battle the commission faced. Nerland was refusing to appear before the commission and had hired a lawyer, Brian Beresh of Edmonton, to help him make his point heard. Nerland had been forced to appear at the Alberta inquiry into the Alberta Aryan Nations/Ku Klux Klan Fest held in Provost in 1990. But in Saskatchewan there were legal obstacles. Unlike Alberta, Saskatchewan inquiries did not have the same legal stature as court trials and therefore could not compel witnesses from other provinces to attend. The Saskatchewan legislature would have to change the law in order to require Nerland to be transported from Stony Mountain Penitentiary in Manitoba.

It should have been a straightforward procedure, but the legislation was inadvertently sidetracked at the committee level. A few days before the politicians were to recess, the Prince Albert newspaper called Myron Kowalsky, MLA for the city, and asked him what had happened to the bill. With only hours to spare, Kowalsky tracked it down and got it passed through the legislature.

The legal blocks were gone, but the game was not over yet. On 5 November, it was announced that the Supreme Court of Canada had refused to hear the application made by the LaChance commission. The inquiry could resume, but it lacked the important ammunition needed to get to the truth about Leo LaChance's death.

On 12 November, the LaChance family and the Prince Albert Tribal Council held a press conference at the Tribal Council's headquarters. Council Chief A. J. Felix, flanked by David LaChance and vice-chiefs Alphonse Bird and John Dantouze, read a news release revealing that the man the RCMP used to spy on the Aryan Nations was none other than Carney Milton Nerland. The Native people had put all their faith in the criminal justice system, Chief Felix said, but that trust had been undermined by the Supreme Court ruling. Now, they would play by the rules of Native justice, that all of the truth be revealed. The inquiry was of great significance to the Native people. Their concerns encompassed not only this one case, but the entire justice system.

The announcement gave further credence to the belief that Nerland was indeed a police informant, and yet the information did not sit well with most people. How could a force as respected as the RCMP have anything to do with as shady and unstable a character as Nerland appeared to be? How could they use as a spy someone careless enough to bring as much attention to himself as Nerland did by killing an Indian?

Informants cannot be people so respectable that they would be out of place in the everyday world of lawbreakers and so unable to gather information on crimes. Nerland, however, was well placed to be able to report on his customers in the gun shop and on the activities of those who embrace white supremacist views. He could tell Mounties what was happening with various racist groups in Canada and the United States.

Why he would want to give the Mounties information is a more interesting question. The money paid to informants is not enough to make the potential danger worthwhile. It is more likely that if Nerland was involved, then he was doing it for kicks: knowing he was playing both sides by being a white supremacist and a spy. His tendency since childhood seems to have been to show off, play a role, attach himself to the trappings of power. What better roles to play than those of Nazi and spy for one of the best-known police forces in the world?

A number of people knew Nerland was the leader of the Saskatchewan branch of the Aryan Nations before he opened his gun shop. Could the fact that he was an informant have assisted him in obtaining a gun shop license? The testimony of the provincial firearms registrar was contradictory. After the murder, he claimed religious and political beliefs are not a reason to reject a license application, yet afterward at the inquiry, the registrar testified that had he known of Nerland's affiliations he would not have granted him a license. Nerland was well-known to immigration officials in 1985, according to an officer who rejected Nerland's attempt to enter the country under the alias Kurt Meyer. The officer testified at the bail hearing that he knew "Meyer" was Nerland. If he was so well-known as a white supremacist, how could the police not know he was involved with the Aryan Nations when he applied for a gun shop license and firearms registrations? If they knew who he was, why did they not act if the firearms registrar is correct and the application could have been rejected? Did he get a license because officials knew he was an Aryan Nations insider and useful to them as well?

Constable Eldon Love, the uniformed officer sent to spy on Nerland by the city police testified he had asked Nerland about going with the gun shop owner to the Provost white supremacist rally. He must have reported the conversation, and if he did, why did Nerland's behaviour in Provost not draw more attention from the city police? Surely at least one saw Nerland's performance on national television.

The testimony of Corporal Lawrence seemed to confirm that Nerland was the informer. Lawrence told the inquiry he returned a call from Nerland at the jail. "I spoke to Mr. Nerland. He said, 'I have no protection here right? I am on my own,' and I said, 'That's right.'" The Mountie went on to say he assumed Nerland wondered if he would have protection from the RCMP and if they would intercede in the investigation. The call would seem to confirm some business relationship between Lawrence and Nerland.

Nerland spoke of threats uttered against him by a leader of the Ku Klux Klan who visited Nerland while he was in Stony Mountain Penitentiary. Why would the klansman threaten Nerland's life if he did not believe Nerland was an informant?

Perhaps the most telling argument for the theory that Nerland is indeed the police informant is the fact that he is now free, in the relative safety of the witness protection plan.

CHAPTER NINETEEN

Nerland:
Neo-Nazi or Not?

At the beginning of the inquiry, Nerland refused to appear. Even after Saskatchewan and Manitoba passed legislation making it possible to compel Nerland to attend the inquiry into LaChance's death and he was transferred from Stony Mountain Penitentiary, outside Winnipeg, to the Saskatchewan Penitentiary he would not testify. It was not until he was charged with contempt that he finally decided to speak.

But — even then — he was determined to control the show. Before he would appear, his lawyer stated his demands: Nerland would not testify before the public; he would not allow his picture to be taken; and he would not allow videos of his testimony to be shown to the public. He would allow the immediate members of the LaChance family to attend his testimony, but not Vice-Chief Alphonse Bird, presumably because Bird and the Prince Albert Tribal Council had held a press conference releasing the information that Carney Nerland was the RCMP informant. Nerland told the inquiry he was threatened daily in the penitentiary and he feared for his life at the hands of Native inmates and members of the Ku Klux Klan. The commissioners agreed to the private testimony, in the interests of Nerland's safety, but insisted on showing the entire tapes to the public, except those parts that might tend to identify the RCMP informant. News photographers would be allowed to take pictures of Nerland and segments of the tape would be available to all television stations. Vice-Chief Bird left voluntarily, although not happily, in order to facilitate the inquiry.

On 6 April 1993, hearings were held in the officers' mess at Saskatchewan Penitentiary, where maximum security could be assured. Nerland was transported to the kitchen loading area by van from inside the prison and then led through the door connecting the kitchen and the inquiry room, RCMP officers in plainclothes preceding and following him. Even though everyone in the room had seen Nerland before, few recognized him until the commissioners spoke to him.

This was a very different Nerland from the one who had appeared in Prince Albert courts two years before. It was a very different Nerland from the neo-Nazi who had bullied and harangued at Provost. It was a very different Nerland from the one who had testified at an Alberta inquiry. His physical appearance had been greatly altered: he had lost over one hundred pounds. Not only was he a different looking man, his persona seemed changed as well. The Carney Nerland who testified before this inquiry was polite, earnest, and helpful — at least most of the time. Now and then, his new image slipped and he replied with sarcasm or parried arrogantly with lawyers who were questioning him. But it was not the Nerland who sneered at police, boasted of his Nazi views, jeered at old men, and bragged in jail.

His new image was bewildering at times: he announced to the inquiry in Prince Albert that in 1985 he had rejected the Ku Klux Klan beliefs. He was no longer a white supremacist. All his actions and statements since his return to Canada from Louisiana in 1985 had been mere role playing, Nerland insisted. The argument did not fit with the facts: that he still devoured everything he could read or watch regarding Hitler, and that he had been visited in penitentiary by other western Canadian white supremacist leaders. And it did not fit with the testimony he gave to the Alberta inquiry in 1991 when he told those commissioners: "I am a National Socialist and that uniform is a National Socialist uniform . . . I'm a Nazi and I was wearing it." At another time, he put it this way, "When I was a serving captain in the

SA of Karl Hand's Nationalist Socialist Liberation Front, I've gone in front of Jewish Defence League members before in violent confrontations in the United States."

Now, a year later, Nerland was telling the Saskatchewan inquiry into the death of Leo LaChance the opposite: that he was not a neo-Nazi or believer in the philosophy of the Church of Jesus Christ Christian Aryan Nations, even though he admitted to being that church's leader in Saskatchewan.

The commission report said it all: "This inquiry does not have the authority to explore the nature and circumstances of [Nerland's] play acting or impersonation [as a white supremacist since 1985]. We do, however, conclude from all the evidence available to us, if Nerland was indeed role-playing, it was an exceedingly comfortable role for him."

Commissioner Peter MacKinnon quietly demonstrated just how easy it was for Nerland to play a part when he drew him into a lengthy dissertation on the man's beliefs about Nazi history. The Nerland who testified at the Alberta inquiry in 1991 that "I don't believe it [the Holocaust] occurred in any way, shape or form, as they present it; that extermination by gassing and cremation was impossible," told the Saskatchewan inquiry the opposite. When MacKinnon asked Nerland who Ernst Kaltenbrunner was, Nerland said Kaltenbrunner was a Gestapo member who was credibly implicated in the extermination of the Jewish race in Europe, thereby admitting that he did actually believe the Holocaust had occurred.

At the inquiry into LaChance's death, the "new" Nerland denied completely that he made the statements the police said he had: that he deserved a medal for shooting an Indian and that he would not eat "Gook" food. No one believed the denials, including the commissioners. Further, they found it inconceivable that he would continue play-acting after LaChance had been shot and he was facing manslaughter charges. They believed Nerland's indifference to the life of Leo LaChance was rooted in deep, very real racism.

Why would Nerland consider being an informant, knowing the

danger from white supremacists if he were found out? How could he suddenly stop being a racist when he had expressed racist beliefs since childhood? Why would he want to inform on an organization that had meant so much to him? Was he feeding the RCMP information with the full knowledge of the Aryan Nations? It is doubtful that he did it for the money. Did it give him a sense of power? A feeling of superiority? None of the crucial questions were answered because the inquiry was not allowed to investigate the matter.

His testimony seemed as sincere as it was unbelievable. How does a gun shop owner come to be playing with a loaded weapon? How could he not know it was loaded? Why did he not find out if LaChance was hit? Why not allow the Good Samaritan to call 911? Why take as many as nine rifles (he could not remember if he took three, six, or nine) with him on a quick trip to Canadian Tire ? Why not talk about the incident with his supportive family with whom he spent several hours? How could he not talk about it? Why not tell his friend Roy McKnight when they drove around for more than an hour? Could they have talked only about the Gulf War? Why was it that McKnight, Nerland, the witnesses, and Nerland's father each told Detective Mesluk they could not pin down times because none wore a watch? Why did Nerland insist on setting the burglar alarm on his shop at 3 A.M. when the shop was guarded front and back by police? What was in the briefcase he wanted so badly to take from the shop that night? Was there really an Aryan Nations membership list or did he want the firearms ledger so no one would know if weapons were missing? What happened to the briefcase? According to police, all that was important from the briefcase was the firearms register and they kept it. The briefcase was given to Roy McKnight, along with all the weapons in the shop. McKnight offered to put up one thousand dollars' bail for Nerland, yet, strangely enough, at the inquiry, Nerland had forgotten McKnight was about to become a partner.

Understandably, David LaChance longed to have Nerland questioned by an all-aboriginal inquiry. "We would have found out the truth. We would have taken as long as it took and we would have gotten the truth." The truth was what David wanted but Nerland's testimony did not even seem to come close to revealing it. In fact, it was very hard to keep Nerland on the subject of the LaChance shooting. He recalled so little about that night. He couldn't remember serving drinks. "I honestly do not recall." He could not recall shooting into the floor that night. "I can't refute what these people say because I do not recall it, oddly enough." He could not remember LaChance being in the shop. "I honestly did not notice the man." He did remember shooting him. "I must have touched the trigger and the weapon went off." He did not think he had ever seen the basement of the shop; the light was burned out, he said. And he did not remember there being a shooting range there. "As far as I remember, no." He explained he got into Brownbridge's car because he forgot he had his own car at the shop. He had been confused by the shot through the door and normally he parked in front where there are meters and not in the back where parking is free. "I took three, six or nine weapons with me." "They were my weapons and I wanted to take them home with me." The three men did drive by Nerland's house but they did not stop to drop off the guns.

Rather than discussing the shooting of Leo LaChance, Nerland wanted to talk about particular police officers. Suddenly, his recall sharpened dramatically and he remembered in great detail racist remarks that he said police officers made to him a year before. He could not remember their names but he pulled six names from his firearms register and began describing conversations he allegedly had had with the officers. Nerland said one policeman had commented, "Those Goddamned Jews and other soulless, mongrel bastards, they got what was coming to them, they shouldn't have showed up at that place [Provost] . . . you looked fantastic there with uniform, jackboots, the dagger and what I especially liked was the shotgun."

But the commissioners and others had difficulty accepting his selective memory and Nerland's attack fizzled out. As Gerry Allbright pointed out, it was the second time that Nerland had deflected attention from himself by blaming others: first the two men in the shop and then the "racist" police.

David had sat at the table with the chiefs during the news conference that had revealed Nerland was a police informer. By bringing it out in the open, they hoped the inquiry could proceed without hindrance. But it did not work out that way. Every time a lawyer asked a question that could conceivably reveal anything about the informer, he was stopped. The right of an informant to privacy had been upheld by the Saskatchewan Court of Appeals and the Supreme Court of Canada. The inquiry obeyed the law scrupulously. Important questions were left unasked: details about racist literature in Nerland's store; for whose benefit had Nerland projected the image of being an Aryan Nations member in his "role-playing"; what political ideology had he then espoused if he was no longer a white supremacist; had he talked to any member of the RCMP after the shooting. No wonder the commissioners had real difficulty with Nerland's credibility.

What worried Nerland in April 1992 were the threats he was receiving from the Ku Klux Klan, the "National Brotherhood" (known in various prisons as Native Awareness Group, Native Brotherhood, or Native Clan), and the Canadian Aryan Brotherhood. Nerland claims the latter is an organization of Aryan members who are incarcerated in Canadian prisons. Prison officials claim not to have heard of it. Whoever they might be, they certainly would not like the idea of Nerland informing on them.

For his protection, he was placed in isolation from other prisoners. Since protective custody is no longer used in the penitentiary system, the administration can, for the good order of the prison or to protect the life of a prisoner, put them in what is called Dissociation, better known as "The Hole." As he feared poison or ground glass in his food, Nerland had become a picky eater and had lost one hundred pounds. He did not have much longer to worry. Shortly after his return to Stony Mountain Penitentiary in April, Nerland was transferred to a minimum security farm institution adjacent to the medium security penitentiary, just north of Winnipeg. In December 1993, Carney Nerland was released on parole, having served two-thirds of his sentence. Under the Witness Protection Act, he received a new name and a new location. Even the LaChance family were not be told where he is. Many people wondered if this was the price paid for his testimony at the inquiry.

CHAPTER TWENTY

The LaChance
Family Speaks

While Leo LaChance's father, Dick, has accepted his son's death and is prepared to move on, he is still angered when the shooting is described as an accident. He does not believe it was an accident. He believes Leo was deliberately shot because he was a Cree. Dick calls it murder.

Dick LaChance now lives in a senior's home in Alberta. He says, "It is very hard for me when a white man killed my boy. It is hard to accept the killing and the way it looks as though the Red Coats (RCMP) are covering up instead of really finding out why. It seems the city police went along with the killer, saying he could go to Alberta [the day after the shooting]. No one knows what he took with him, books? guns? to put away at his Dad's place. He had no problem to go there with everything [connected to the Aryan Nations].

"Why was everything so slow? If it was an Indian who shot some-one, in half an hour he would be locked up and not go any place. Eve-rything Nerland asked, people went along with. It seemed like there was a plan with the killer, the witnesses, the Royal Canadian Mounted Police and the justice system to put everything in order to look like an accident. The lawyers were very soft on Nerland and the witnesses. No one was saying very much. I think all the witnesses should be thrown in jail until they tell the truth!

"When the treaty was signed, they said there would be an Indian agent there to help us always, to make sure we are not cheated. There was no Indian agent there to make sure we were not cheated of justice.

"I don't accept the inquiry report. The family has been cheated. It is very hard to forget and go in a different direction now. Justice was not done. It is hard to leave it. I know [the witnesses] were lying!"

David LaChance had fought for an inquiry so the truth of his brother's death would be revealed. The restrictions on what questions could be asked at the inquiry, especially those related to Nerland as an informant, were frustrating to David, because the answers were crucial to learning the truth. When the commission released its report in November 1993, David said he was not satisfied and he would release his own when he had examined the official findings. He believes much was covered up by the police and the lawyers, as well as by the witnesses and Nerland himself. In November 1994, he made public the following document:

Cult Compound Pawn Shop,
River Street West,
Prince Albert, Saskatchewan.
Carney Nerland – Aryan Nations Leader
    – R.C.M.P. Informant

Police, Government of Saskatchewan workers and Aryan Nations people meet inside the pawn shop with Carney Nerland, on a regular basis.

On January 28, 1991, Leo LaChance was walking by the pawn shop. He was invited to go in the pawn shop by a group of men. He was shot by one of the men. Another shot was fired through the door to make it look accidental.

The "soft" investigations began. On January 29, 1991, Carney Nerland had no problems by police. Carney Nerland was allowed to leave Prince Albert, Saskatchewan to travel to Alberta.

Carney Nerland was to take guns, shells, Aryan Nations ledger, tear gas and other important things to his friends, other Aryan Nations leaders, in Alberta, for safekeeping.

On January 30, 1991, Regina, Saskatchewan RCMP came to Prince Albert. The RCMP member from Regina met the [city] police and the Crown. He informed them Carney Nerland was the RCMP informant.

In other words, "Take it easy on Carney Nerland."

Police and John Fields, Crown, layed [*sic*] the manslaughter charge instead of the murder charge! From that moment on, everything was a cover-up.

Whoever pulled the trigger deserves life in prison. Also, the other people who lied are evil people. They should be put in prison for a long time.

No justice was done.

Me and my friends are working hard to have the case reopened.

My brother, Leo LaChance died in pain, but not forgotten.

Leo's brother

David LaChance.

The Prince Albert Tribal Council also announced that it was unhappy with the commission's report and that it intended to carry out its own investigation and prepare its own report.

The federal government delivered the final blow in a stunning announcement 24 November 1993. Nerland would not only be released from prison, he would be protected. The family that had quietly and with dignity asked for the truth concerning the killing of their brother Leo was left without knowledge of where Nerland might be or if he meant to kill another of its members. Nerland, who showed contempt and callous disregard for the life of Leo LaChance, was to be protected from all harm. The family that suffered four deaths and the disappearance of a fifth member was to be left exposed. Nerland, who took one of those lives, was to be hidden away by the government from his supposed enemies. The taxpayers who paid nearly half a million dollars to learn Nerland was an uncaring killer could now pay the expense of keeping him safe.

Above Leo LaChance's grave in the small cemetery on the reserve, his brother Albert has placed a cross he fashioned himself out of diamond willow. On it hangs Leo's favourite baseball cap. Below it is a small jar to hold offerings of tobacco, sacred to the Cree. His elderly father hopes that someday there will be enough money for a small headstone and a picket fence to protect his son's grave.

At the feast marking the first anniversary of Leo's death, his father addressed the people gathered together: "I have no bitter words for anyone after the death of my son. I pray daily for peace among our nations, Native and non-Native, and especially for the young people of both nations. I pray for healing. I pray for the future. I hope this gathering will mark the beginning of the healing process.

"Put an end to your mourning and go forward from the turning point this ceremony marks. I want us all to wake up tomorrow in good spirits and carry on, knowing my son is in a good place. I have no bitterness toward Prince Albert or toward my son's killer. This ceremony asks a blessing on both families: the Nerlands and the LaChances."

CHAPTER TWENTY-ONE

The Inquiry Report

After twenty-five days of testimony from forty-one witnesses over eighteen months, the commission of inquiry into the death of Leo LaChance released a seventy-five-page report of its findings and recommendations.

The Prince Albert *Daily Herald* editorial that appeared in the newspaper the first day of the inquiry set the tone adopted for the report. While, it said, Nerland's sentence could not be extended, there would be the opportunity to learn about the case. The police, courts and prosecutors would have a chance to explain what they did and why.

"Nerland's sentence cannot be extended no matter how fair that might seem to some. The charges against Nerland cannot be changed now. He cannot be tried at this point for the murder of Leo LaChance.

"What the inquiry can do is see to it all the information about the case is provided by the witnesses and the police. . . .

"If they were wrong, the commission can say so. It can't change what happened. But it can make recommendations for future action."

And so it did.

After the commissioners and the lawyers for all of the interested parties had had an opportunity to examine and cross-examine all of the witnesses, the commission arrived at conclusions about what had happened the night Leo LaChance was killed. But because no questions could be asked that would identify the informant, the commission did not learn all that had happened that night.

Was he shot inside the store or not? The commission was unsure. Was it an accident as Nerland and the judicial system said or was it a racist murder as the LaChance family and others believe? The commission did not come up with a definite answer. It criticized the police for not recognizing at the time that racism may have been the motivating factor for Nerland's actions. The police should have looked into Nerland's activities as a white supremacist. There should have been a more careful investigation of where Nerland and LaChance were when the fatal shot was fired. It might have made the difference between murder and manslaughter, the commissioners said.

The police also came under criticism for having allowed Nerland to have a license to sell firearms. When the license was first issued in 1989, Nerland met the criteria and police said his Aryan Nations connections were not known. By 1990, however, those connections were known to city police officers and certainly to the RCMP. However, not all of the police had been informed. Corporal Lawrence of the RCMP testified he did not know if the city police had been kept aware of Nerland's doings. He just collected the information. He did not disseminate it. There were city police who knew about Nerland's political leanings and some who knew nothing.

But Nerland still met the criteria. He did not have a criminal record, a record of a mental disorder, or a history of behaviour that involved violence or threats of violence. The license for 1991 was in the mail when authorities learned that a shipment of stun guns addressed to Nerland had been seized by customs. Nerland denied knowledge of them and they were returned to the sender. The provincial firearms registrar did not indicate the license was in jeopardy, just that it should be monitored. On 21 January 1991, ten days before LaChance was shot at the gunshop, the license for 1992 was on the desk of the provincial firearms registrar, with all the criteria met for issue.

The firearms business license was legal, but was it right? The commission did not think so. In its opinion, anyone with Nerland's background and association is unsuitable to obtain a license. The provincial firearms registrar, Al Terry, testified at the inquiry that knowledge about Nerland's membership in the Aryan Nations and what that organization stood for was relevant. The city police were criticized for not looking into the matter more fully and for not telling Terry what they had learned. The commission believed knowledge of Nerland's behaviour in Provost, Alberta, might well have meant denying Nerland a license.

"If our conclusion that the information available in this regard 'would have provided compelling reason to revoke Nerland's [firearms] business permit' is correct, it follows that the Northern Pawn and Gun Shop should not have been open for business on 28 January 1991."

The police argue that, at the time of the shooting, Nerland was operating on the original license, issued in March 1990. It did not expire until 31 January 1991, three days after the shooting. It was in effect, and had been for seven months, when the Provost Aryan Nations Fest was held. The provincial firearms registrar had said in an interview in 1991, before the inquiry, that membership in a church, which is how the Aryan Nations are considered in Canada, could not prevent the granting of a firearms registration. The law has since been changed. The Prince Albert Police Department was notified 26 July 1994 that in future: "it is requested that when assessing the background on any applicant for a Firearms Acquisition Certificate (FAC) or Firearms Business Permit, that any information, or intelligence, indicating association with individuals or organizations advocating hatred, violence or a propensity for violence, such as, but not limited to, racist organizations or motor cycle gangs, be communicated to my office with the application."

The Crown prosecutors had made the right charge, given the information they had, the commissioners concluded. But they should have looked deeper and longer into the motivation for the shooting by ordering further investigation of Nerland's Aryan Nations activity. They should also have looked more closely at the evidence on whether LaChance was inside or outside the door when he was shot. Defense lawyer Earl Kalenith had told the judge that racism had nothing to do with the shooting, but if the prosecutors had been able to substantiate accusations of racism against Nerland, then the sentencing judge would have been able to increase the penalty. No fault could be attached to the judge, they added. Racism had had a great deal to do with the shooting of Leo LaChance and the police and prosecutors should have investigated this angle in depth.

The commissioners did not find any evidence that the police and prosecutors had "gone soft" on Nerland, but they did find that police and prosecutors had not investigated hard enough to solve the crime.

"Racism is a complicated phenomenon and people whose duty it is to serve the public in a multiracial society must understand it. To this end, it is our recommendation that the level of cross-cultural training of police and prosecutors be increased and improved in the interests of fuller understanding of the dynamics of racism."

Specifically, the commissioners said the police department should have a Cree-speaking officer on duty at all times and that such an officer should have accompanied LaChance in the ambulance from the Prince Albert hospital to the Saskatoon hospital. It is a peculiar bit of reverse racism that no one learned the white officer who was with LaChance is a Cree speaker capable of understanding LaChance had he spoken Cree that night. LaChance spoke only English, even when muttering in pain. The force has since hired a teacher to offer voluntary instruction to the members, but few have taken advantage of the opportunity. Shortly before municipal elections were held in 1994, four new officers were hired to meet a shortfall of several years' duration. None were Cree speaking. Since then, four other officers, including a Cree speaker, have retired or resigned, leaving the force without one Native Cree speaker. There are four white officers who speak Cree. There are no immediate plans to bring the force up to strength. In a city with a population one-third aboriginal, it is not seen to be enough.

The mayor and council in place throughout the LaChance affair have been replaced and the new members hope to implement a new philosophy of action against racism.

The commissioners did not find evidence of organized racism in Prince Albert, but they agreed that racism was a big factor in the killing. "When the 'wrongs' that we have identified are viewed in the light of our finding that those responsible for those 'wrongs' acted throughout with integrity, objectiveness and good faith, what is the explanation for what occurred?

"It became apparent to us during the hearings that we are still a long way from being a tolerant society. Living as we do in widely separated areas of our country, we see this as a Canadian problem — not just a local one. In our view, the goal of achieving a society of tolerance, understanding and cross-cultural respect and sensitivity will not be reached until minority cultures are recognized, accepted and appreciated by the majority culture in this country. We believe the majority culture in our society does not understand the extent of the impact of racism on those who are its victims.

"The leading investigators and prosecutors from whom we heard evidence are people of integrity and good faith, but they did not understand either the ways in which racism may have explained Nerland's behaviour or the reasons why the people who themselves have experienced racism might have serious concerns and questions about the way in which the Nerland case was handled.

"Clearly, the experience of the Indian and Métis people is that the criminal justice system discriminates against them. The historical record supports their view. If they do not see justice done, they have good reason to believe justice has not been done. If, because there is a guilty plea, there is neither a trial not a preliminary inquiry into a case that raises significant public concern, great care should be taken by the representatives of the Crown to ensure all relevant circumstances are not only carefully explored, but are also made known to the public."

The commissioners criticized, but they also praised. They applauded the attitudes and sincerity of the police and prosecutors, the cooperation between civic and aboriginal leaders in the community, the attitude that the two peoples must and will continue to coexist in Prince Albert. The coming together will come from within the community, not from outside, they insisted.

Epilogue

While in Prince Albert, Reverend James Nisbet listed the birth place of his converts in the baptismal register as "on the prairies." Bernice Sayese's birth certificate is a little more precise. It gives range, township, and line numbers, the western Canadian means of identifying places on the open prairies. In her case, it locates a log home in the bush north of Kinistino, a district known as Strong Pine.

Bernice is a Métis woman who moved to Prince Albert with her parents and her eight brothers and sisters when she was four. It was there she learned about racism. She clearly remembers begging her mother to attend a public school parent-teacher night. Her mother did not want to go but she did anyway, to please Bernice. She was the only Native woman there. People stared.

It is very different now for Bernice and her children. They are involved in a community school dedicated to helping children and parents learn about each other. The mixing of races is a constant occurrence, and not just during sports events as it was in Bernice's school days. Her children do not have to feel "different" and therefore inferior. Bernice quit high school in grade ten because her clothes were so shabby that she stood out and was made to feel bad. Her children will not have to face that experience. Their chances of staying in school and getting a high school diploma are much better.

In 1974, Bernice took a job with the Native Women's Counselling and Referral Centre and began on-the-job training in social work that led to the profession she has carried on ever since. Today she is coordinator of the Mayor's Committee on Race Relations. Sayese's office is in City Hall on the main street of Prince Albert. From there, she can see how visible the problem of racism is.

The death of Leo LaChance made people think about racial attitudes and this was heightened during the inquiry. The concern has continued and the Mayor's Committee is helping to make changes. Sayese says Natives are included on more boards, including the Chamber of Commerce and they are no longer considered "tokens." Vice-Chief Eugene Arcand of the Federation of Saskatchewan Indian Nations can take some of the credit. He has urged Natives either to voice their opinions on the boards they join or resign from them.

The mayor's committee, established by former mayor Gordon Kirkby, now the member of parliament for the area, is in the process of setting up a crosscultural resource group. The dozen members will undergo training and then educate resource people from many different organizations. The resource people, in turn, will teach crosscultural courses to their own staffs.

Memorial Square lies between City Hall and Central Avenue, a mixture of broad walks, flowerbeds, and grass. It is flanked by the old City Hall, now an art centre, and a war memorial. Benches are scattered along the edges of the square. Across the square from the war memorial facing Central Avenue is a rather forbidding statue of John Diefenbaker, the great prime minister from Prince Albert. He stares sternly downwards while pointing an accusing finger at those in the public square at his feet. Diefenbaker inadvertently helped these people decline to their pitiful state by allowing Indians to purchase liquor. But Diefenbaker can hardly be blamed. Many of the people at his feet, passed out or stumbling across the square, cannot afford liquor anyway. These are the poor and hopeless, the slum dwellers and the people who come to town early each day and drown themselves in solvent abuse and cheap alcoholic concoctions from household products. These are the stereotypes, the people who are seen, the people with nothing to do and nowhere to go and no hope of anything different.

A subcommittee on solvent abuse has been set up to attempt to ban the ready availability of glue, gasoline, hairspray, Lysol, and Listerine, substances that are passports to insensibility and eventually death. The Indian Métis Friendship Centre offers what it can but there is only one worker for the two- to three-hundred serious cases of substance abuse per month.

There is another serious problem facing the city. In Memorial Square and in the downtown mall, there are packs of young children with nothing to do. Very occasionally an adult will sharply admonish them for the way they talk to their elders but this lack of respect on the part of youths from both nations is a real concern. Young white youths freely admit there are beatings of Native youths and older people downtown and in the areas of town where Natives tend to live. Until people feel better about themselves, respect will be hard to find, and respect is the key word in Bernice Sayese's vocabulary. She does not want to think what the city could be like in the future if youths are not taught respect and instead are allowed to continue to roam like a pack of wild animals.

Ex-inmates and parolees also loiter at the malls and on the downtown streets. The Friendship Centre offers counselling and a healing circle. But Sayese sees a far better means of helping all of the hopeless people. There is a real need for a shelter, a place to dry out and a place to be safe for awhile. People need help getting temporary employment that could lead to full-time jobs. Assessment programs are needed. There is a great deal of work to do.

Twice now, *Chatelaine* magazine has listed Prince Albert as one of the ten best places in Canada to live, and with good reason. It is a small, pretty city of clean streets and parks, clean air and clean water. The surrounding area is spectacularly beautiful and housing is affordable. A three- or four-bedroom modern home in a good neighbourhood can be bought for eighty-five thousand dollars. There are starter homes for less and magnificent homes on acreages for under two hundred thousand dollars. There are gracious old homes, including Keyhole Castle, overlooking the city from the South Hill. Cottage country at a dozen popular lake resorts is an hour or less away. Hunting and fishing are abundant. Hockey is king, but teams in nearly every sport have gone on to the nationals year after year. The Vickers School band has won gold medals at the national music fest annually and there is an internationally renowned boys' choir. There are art shows and dinner theatres and Amy's on Second, regularly listed as one of the best places in Canada to dine.

There are still fur traders on River Street, but Prince Albert no longer depends on them or even on the river for its economic base. Weyerhaeuser Canada Ltd. operates a pulp and paper mill with a work force of eight hundred. More than one thousand people are employed by the three penitentiaries, two jails, and related work camps and youth camps. There are plenty of agriculture-related and service industries and small businesses.

People like it here and they took the shooting death of Leo LaChance seriously. They fought back and demanded to know the facts. They acknowledged their prejudices and that racism exists and they are proud of the changes that are being made. Leo LaChance did not die in vain.

Still, one question haunts this city: What really happened that night when there was a shooting down on River Street?